The Way of the Activist

By
Jamie Driscoll
&
Rachel Broadbent

First edition.
First published in United Kingdom[1], 2017

Please feel free to contact us.
We would be happy to help in any way we can.

Contact
Facebook: /TalkSocialism
Email: talksocialismwebsite@gmail.com
Website: www.talksocialism.com

[1] Still part of the European Union

CONTENTS

INDEX OF SIDEBARS

Introduction

Education is the most powerful weapon which you can use to change the world.

- Nelson Mandela

INTRODUCTION

It's an exciting time - socialism is back on the mainstream political agenda. Hundreds of thousands of people have joined political movements because they want to build a world with sustainable economic prosperity and a world that doesn't squander the talents and life chances of millions. They want to see an end to spin doctors, media lies, tax dodging corporations and people being treated as disposable economic units.

But how? It's daunting - there seem to be so many fronts to fight on, and so many causes to support. We need a formula that allows people to make a difference without getting burned out.

What makes a difference in the long term - more than anything else - is that people are able to explain the WHY of socialism. Most people with a shred of compassion get the idea that a fairer world would be a good thing. But unless we can explain HOW that is possible we'll struggle to get past the legions of billionaire-owned media outlets that want to make politics about personalities and mudslinging.

That's what we're advocating: talk to people. Learn the basics of participatory politics, how to get people involved in a sustainable way. How to cut through the economic jargon and red-herrings about "magic money trees". The first task is to get just a few tens of thousands of people able to explain these ideas in the course of their everyday lives, to family, friends and work colleagues. If we can do that, the political narrative changes. The ideas of socialism will be widespread. Ordinary people will have heard them undiluted by tabloids.

The ideas of economists and political philosophers are more powerful than is widely understood. Indeed, the world is ruled by little else. Politicians come and politicians go. Even those who are just in it for personal ambition are enacting one economic or political theory in preference to another. As soon as we get the ideas of modern, 21st century socialism widely discussed, a new layer of politicians and activists will be able to make them the default, common sense choice.

Who is a socialist?

You might not self-identify as a socialist. No problem - we're using it as a shorthand for anyone who wants to see a world where public policy is about sustainable economic prosperity for all, where diplomatic solutions are preferred to war, where long-term social development is put before short term profit. Above all, a socialist believes that people achieve more when they share and cooperate than when they try to keep everything for themselves through destructive competition. If you can sign up to that, this book is for you, and we're happy if you call yourself an environmentalist, an anti-poverty campaigner or just a decent, honest person.

How to Use This Book

The chapters are deliberately short, to maximise accessibility. They assume no prior knowledge at all. You can dip in and out, or read it cover to cover.

It is also designed to support a discussion or reading group. You could choose a chapter as a starter to a political discussion. It's also designed to be a distilled source of political experience. The sections on social psychology and political activism are a good place to start if you're looking for ideas on how to get more people involved in your campaign or organisation.

The book is divided into four sections: social psychology, political philosophy, economics, and participatory politics. Even if you're an experienced activist, there should be something new for you, if only to hear what you already know explained in a new way.

So who are we?

Talk Socialism is a group of political activists who are spreading the ideas found in this book. In particular, we are trying to raise the bar on how to communicate these ideas.

INTRODUCTION

We started in Newcastle, and now have friends and contributors across the UK (and some overseas). We're not a political party, or a faction, and we don't have a detailed political programme. Instead we work with other groups and charities, including the Labour Party, to help people clarify their own thinking, come to a better collective understanding, and combine good ideas from the social sciences and fashion them into tools to help with their political organising and campaigning.

We are non-dogmatic; if you're a social democrat, Red, Blue or Purple Labour, Momentum or Fabian, Green Party or SNP, libertarian socialist, Marxist, Trotskyist, we won't tell you you're wrong for the views you're holding. Our most important rule is that our sessions and publications are positive, participatory, and fun.

We run lots of training sessions throughout the country, and reading groups and some towns and cities have regular workshop sessions. Everything we do is based on the ideas in this book. All of our training sessions work in harmony with what we know about people: we work with human nature[2], not against it. A big part of that is having fun; Talk Socialism workshops are always interesting and usually funny, and involve people doing things. Politics is about people, it's not a spectator sport.

If you're reading this book, there's a good chance you're already actively working to bring about a better world. Hopefully what you read will give you some new tools to be more effective. But the people we really want to reach are those who want to change things, but don't know where to start. If you're one of those people: hello! Read the book in any order you like. Then get onto the Internet and look at the Talk Socialism website. See when the next activity is taking place, and come along and meet us. The world will only change if you do something to change it.

[2] Or nurture, if you prefer

Psychology

The greatest discovery of my generation is that human beings can alter their lives by altering their attitudes of mind.

- William James

If, as socialists[3], we want to persuade people to organise society in a better way, and we want to build political organisations and movements to do that, then we have to take account of how people actually behave, rather than how we would like them to behave.

We all have an instinctive understanding for how people behave, but it's often a mix of personal experience, cultural expectations, and a mix of both wishful and pessimistic thinking. Few of us are in the habit of checking the evidence to see how behavioural changes actually occur in real groups of people.

Social psychology looks at how people behave as a result of their interactions with other people. It is distinct from clinical psychology, studies of cognition and consciousness, psychoanalysis, developmental psychology and other branches, which tend to look from the perspective of the individual. It's particularly relevant to socialism because it provides an evidence base for how people are likely to change their behaviour and opinions as result of political activities. It gives insights into what motivates them to vote or accept certain ideas and ideologies as desirable.

[3] Or however you self identify.

Knowledge Illusion

Never argue with stupid people, they will drag you down to their level and beat you with experience.

- Greg King

In 1995 a man called McArthur Wheeler robbed two banks at gunpoint in Pittsburgh, in broad daylight with his face uncovered. The security footage was broadcast on the news that night, and he was arrested an hour later. When he asked the police how they found him, he was amazed, and said, "But I wore the juice!" He had rubbed lemon juice on his face, and thought that because lemon juice works as invisible ink, it would hide his face from the security cameras.

This led social psychologists David Dunning and Justin Kruger to wonder why someone so inept could have the confidence to rob a bank. They performed a series of experiments, which have since been extended to cover everything from grammar, telling jokes, playing chess or driving a car. They found that people who score very poorly on the tests,

1. Overestimated their own level of skill,
2. Failed to recognise genuine skill in others.

As Dunning said, "If you're incompetent, you can't know you're incompetent. . . . The skills you need to produce a right answer are exactly the skills you need to recognise what a right answer is."

People got less confident as they gained a little genuine skill in a subject, and only became as confident as the ignorant when they actually were genuinely quite skilled.

Everyone has seen this, whether it's a demotivational manager at work who thinks she's a great leader or an idiot zipping through traffic because he thinks he has the skills of a racing driver.

So don't feel bad if you think someone is an ignorant fool. As Marx[4] famously said, "He may look like an idiot and talk like an idiot but don't let that fool you. He really is an idiot." Everyone's opinion is not equally valid. In a 2014 survey on whether the US should intervene in Ukraine, the people most strongly supportive

---

[4] Groucho

of military action were the ones least able to identify it on a map. But how can you be sure that you're not an overconfident idiot?

Two more researchers, Frank Keil and Leonid Rozenblit, wanted to test how people could be made aware of their limitations. They developed a test that asked people to rate their own understanding of everyday phenomena, whether it was how a bicycle works, or how a toilet flushes. Subjects were asked to rate themselves on their understanding, from 1 (complete ignorance) to 7 (complete knowledge). Not surprisingly, most people score themselves highly on knowing how a bicycle works. They then got the participants to write down, in detail, how the various mechanisms worked, including gear shifts, brakes, transfer of forces, and so on, then asked them to rate their understanding on the seven point scale again. They found that many people who had rated themselves highly gave a much lower rating the second time, but those who actually did know a lot about the subject - as determined by their answers - rated themselves the same before and after being asked.

Keil and Rozenblit concluded that people subconsciously changed the question from "how well do you understand..." to "how familiar are you with..." Everyone had seen bikes since childhood, so assumed they knew all about them. Only when asked to explain it did they spot their own lack of knowledge.

Building on this, Steve Sloman and Philip Fernbach tested the same idea in the field of politics. Using subjects like Obamacare, tax rates and environmental policy, they asked people to rate their approval or disapproval of specific policies on a scale of 1 = strongly agree, 4 = neutral, to 7 = strongly disagree. They then asked people to generate a causal explanation of what would be required to implement the policy, how it would work in detail in practise, and its various effects. They then asked people to rate approval or disapproval again, and found that those with very strong opinions (1 or 7) tended to be much more moderate in their views when they could not generate detailed explanations.

By comparison, they did a similar experiment, but this time, instead of asking people to generate a detailed cause-and-

PINT & POLITICS

One of the workshops we deliver most often is called A Pint & Politics. It's a role-play using forum theatre, where one of us acts the role of Joe (or Jo), an average citizen who has been exposed to the various media and cultural narratives about economics, lazy benefit scroungers, Labour crashing the economy in 2008, and so on. Then the participants feed lines to another actor who is playing the role of Joe's friend, in an attempt to get Joe to think more positively about socialism.

As well as being great fun, it's always fascinating to see the participants make a similar journey, as they come to discover that tackling Joe head-on is counterproductive, and telling him that he needs to realise something about corporate tax evasion or that Tory newspapers are owned by millionaires has little effect. But when they ask him how does he think certain policies - socialist or neoliberal - would play out in practice, he starts to become much more open minded. They get him to use system 2 - slow thinking (see the chapter: Thinking Fast and Slow).

effect explanation of the policy implementation, they asked people to write down their reasons for their opinion. This time, when asked to rate their approval or disapproval after giving reasons, they found that people were even more committed to their strong opinions than previously.

When asked to explain the causal effects of a policy, people became more aware of gaps in their knowledge. But if asked why they support something, they provide a whole list of independent justifications, based on values, sound bites, prejudices and circular arguments.

Knowing this, we can be better communicators. If you want to change a person's opinion on a subject, don't ask them why they believe what they do: they'll just recall all their affirmative reasons. Instead, ask them if they can explain what the consequences would be, in practice, in detail. That way they'll become more aware of the gaps in their knowledge, and more open minded. Don't ask people why they believe something, ask them how it works.

Group Dynamics

What I know most surely about morality and the duty of mankind, I owe to sport and I learned it playing football.

- Albert Camus

Everyone's heard of group dynamics. We know from personal experience that people sometimes work well together, and sometimes don't, but few of us are familiar enough with a conceptual framework to explain why that's so (at least without blaming someone).

We tend to view the groups we're part of from a very subjective perspective. We have our own reasons for joining and remaining in groups (even if we're unaware of them) whether those groups are families, social circles, political organisations, or workplaces. We form opinions about our fellows, often with a good degree of empathy and understanding, and are predisposed to think of the group's success as being the sum total of the group's individual efforts.

Group dynamics takes a different perspective. Rather than evaluate the individuals and their levels of ability, motivation and personalities, it looks at the interdependence of goals, and recognises that the structure of a group affects its members. Structure in this sense is not just the written rules, but the operating culture and agreed or implied group norms. Most of us have been in meetings of a very formal nature, where people speak through the chair and discussion occurs as a series of short speeches; other meetings are more fluid and operate like a dialogue, back and forth, with questions, responses, and even banter. This is part of the group structure, even if it's just "the way we've always done it".

The social psychologist Kurt Lewin coined the term Group Dynamics in a 1947 article. According to Lewin, interdependence of goals is the primary factor in whether a group is successful - not individual motivation or the ability of its members.

Interdependence of goals means that you need other members of the group to achieve your objectives. It doesn't mean everyone has precisely the same goals, just that they are mutually reinforcing. Running is something anyone can do on her own, yet there are many successful running clubs. Some members might need the peer pressure and support to get out there, some experienced members might derive satisfaction from helping beginners, some might need the security of running in a group on dark winter nights. The point is, the dynamic is mutually reinforcing: by pursuing their own goal, they also help others achieve theirs. In time, members adopt a set of group norms that crystallise into a structure that reinforces these behaviours. In the case of a running club, it might be the norm to assign an old hand to run alongside a beginner, or something as simple as going for a drink afterwards.

Whatever the nature of the group, if you can achieve your goals without help from anyone else, you'll probably drift away from the group. In a workplace environment where people can't drift away because group attendance is compulsory, motivation plummets and contribution to the group will be very low. In a voluntary collaboration, whether sports club or political campaign, people will vote with their feet.

Members of political groups still have all the usual human goals - banter, friendship, enjoying responsibility, altruism. But the goals that define a group as being political are usually much more distant. Ending racism, achieving nuclear disarmament, or eradicating poverty are not things that any one of us can do, so we need to band together. But, they're not objectives we're likely to achieve as local groups either: the problems are so vast and systemic, and need society-wide change.

So unless there's some concrete progress towards that political goal that people feel can be achieved by attending their local group, they tend to remain paper members and pay their subs; they get their human interaction elsewhere. That, in a nutshell, is why so many Labour Party members don't attend branch meetings: they don't think running through minutes and matters arising will make a Labour government any more likely. (Be honest: do you think that unless your branch functions, the Labour Party won't win power?)

So if you want a political group to be successful, it has to help people achieve goals in a way that they can't on their own. A sure sign that groups have people pursuing goals that are not interdependent is when splits and bickering occur. That's not to say that personality clashes don't exist, and some people just really are hard work; but when people have a clear shared objective, they tend to unite.

In political groups, though, people often have agendas and habits of operating that are very different from others in the group. Some want to advance an ideology dogmatically, some want to engage in public protest, some want to build organisational structures, some want direct action, some want to pass resolutions, some want to support community initiatives, some want to get press and publicity for a cause. For that reason alone, it's often worth deciding: what precisely are we trying to achieve? What is the objective that we can all agree on, that we can actually make some progress on in the foreseeable future? If the goal is vast and distant (like ending poverty), then collectively agree on a constituent goal that at least represents real progress on a small scale. If you can't do great things, do small things in a great way. United we stand, divided we fall.

All of this probably seems quite obvious. But very few political groups do it.

Group Development

If you're setting up a new project or campaign, you should be realistic about how well a new team can perform. In 1965, Educational Psychologist Bruce Tuckman identified four stages all teams go through: Forming, Storming, Norming, and Performing[5].

Forming: The team meets or coalesces. People are expectant, polite, and unsure of roles and responsibilities. Detailed goals and operating practises are unclear. Knowledge of the rest of the team is lacking, and communication is slow and cumbersome because there is not yet a strong shared frame of reference. Most members tend to look to people in positions of authority for a guide on appropriate group norms. The main risk at this stage is that the group stays in the abstract planning stage and doesn't get on with the task at hand.

---

[5] It rhymes so it must be true

Storming: Members have started to form opinions of progress so far, and of other members. Different ideas may compete for ascendancy and if badly managed this phase can be very destructive for the team. Often, members voice opinions on the character and integrity of other participants, and allege that others are shirking responsibility or attempting to dominate. This can be down to personality clashes and differences in working style, or to having different objectives for the group. Disagreements and personality clashes must be resolved before the team can progress out of this stage. Tolerance of each team member and their differences should be emphasised.

A balance has to be struck: too much emphasis on consensus and avoidance of conflict may produce plans that are half-baked or ineffective. Strong facilitative leadership is required to avoid this. Some groups never make it out of the storming phase.

Norming: If the group resolves its disputes, then norms of behaviour are established, roles are accepted, and goals are clarified. People are willing to agree to disagree, and focus on the common goals. Often, people come to appreciate the strengths of other members and see their perspective. Norming and storming can often overlap, as new external tasks and challenges cause the group to repeat previous storming behaviour.

The risk in the norming phase is setting into a rut; fear of "rocking the boat" can inhibit creativity and drive, and avoid facing up to controversial decisions.

Performing: Once group norms and roles are established, group members focus on achieving common goals, and often reach a high level of success. Group knowledge is high, communication links are strong. Tasks allocating and decision making is collaborative, people are given substantial autonomy over working practises; dissent is expected and encouraged, and there is a high level of trust and respect between members. Sounds lovely, doesn't it?

Diffusion of Innovation

The difficulty lies not so much in developing new ideas, as in escaping from old ones.

- John Maynard Keynes

It's kind of obvious that everything we take for granted now must have been a new idea at some time. Some ideas spread and catch on, others seem promising at first, but seem to lose momentum and disappear. The same cultural dynamics apply whether it's the spread of a new academic theory, the adoption of new products, or people changing to new operating procedures. As socialists, they way ideas spread through a social network determines our success.

In 1962, sociologist Everett Rogers published a theory called the **Diffusion of Innovations**. He had accumulated studies as diverse as whether farmers planted new kinds of crops, the success of health campaigns to boil drinking water, and introduction of ethics codes to schools. In his words, "Diffusion is essentially a social process through which people talking to people spread an innovation."

As an innovation spreads through a population it is adopted by different sub-groups in a definite order. Rogers labelled these groups innovators, early adopters, early majority, late majority, and laggards.

Innovators are keen to adopt new ideas, and almost pride themselves on being ahead of the curve (at least within a specific field of culture: e.g. technology, or fashion, or political ideology - it's possible to be an Innovator in technology and a Laggard in fashion.) They are willing to take risks on trying new ideas and products, partly because they're knowledgeable about the field, which in turn makes it less risky for them. If you're a tech wizard, your skill means that trying out a new email system doesn't involve a lot of upheaval the way it would for most people. Typically, Innovators make up just 2.5% of a social system, and they often try new things simply because they get a buzz from it.

Early Adopters generally have a reputation for being "in the know" amongst a social system. Other people tend to look to them to keep up to date. They tend to adopt an innovation because they can see the potential for its use. Early Adopters represent about 13% of a social system.

The **Early Majority** are those people who only adopt an idea once it has "caught on". They don't adopt an innovation because of what it might do in future, but because it makes life easier for them right now. About 34% of people are Early Majority.

The **Late Majority** are generally sceptical about change. They only adopt an innovation when the average group member has already done so, and because it's become the way things are done now. These are the people who cannot be persuaded to try something new until they've seen loads of other people do it first. The Late Majority mirrors the Early Majority in numbers, being about 34% of the members of any group or society.

Finally, the **Laggards**, at about 16% of a group, are those who will never adopt an innovation until there's no choice, usually because the old way of doing things no longer exists.

By the way, if you're reading this book, you're probably an Innovator or an Early Adopter in a political context.

This can be plotted on a bell-curve.

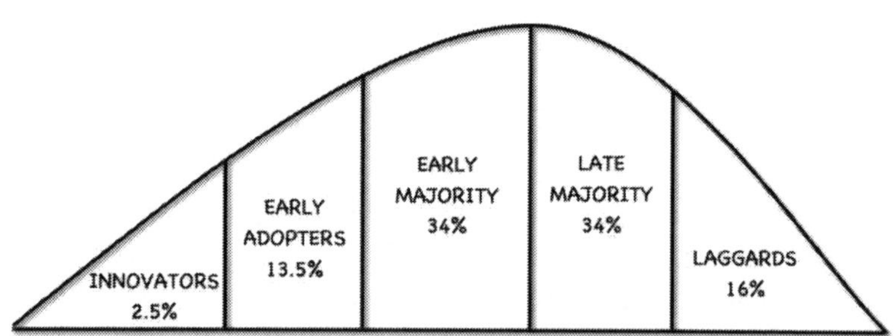

The key point is that one group is only persuaded after the more innovative group has adopted a new product or procedure. The people who think like Early Majority types won't be persuaded by Innovators. They regard these people as too experimental, and possibly not grounded in real world pragmatic results. But if an Early Adopter talks to an Early Majority person, he might listen, because the Early Adopter has a reputation for good judgement on the matter, and isn't excited about the innovation's features, but about how the innovation is useful.

There's a **Chasm** between Early Adopters and Early Majority. Unless an idea bridges the gap between Early Adopters and Early Majority, it will fail to gain a critical mass and its diffusion will stall. This is true for political ideas and organisations as much as for online shopping or mobile phones.

Too often political activists, as Innovators, try to convince everyone they encounter in their network (e.g. Trade Union, or local Labour Party) to join a campaign or set up an event, only to find it a frustrating experience. It's not that people don't agree with your goals, it's just they judge its practical value differently from you.

If you want to change an organisation

TWO-STEP FLOW THEORY

Communication spreads through networks. Advertisers would have us believe we bought iPhones because we saw the adverts. But mostly, it's because we've seen other people using iPhones and asked them about them.

The Two-Step Flow theory of communication models this approach. Media makes information available, but most people base their opinion on how other people react to that information. This applies equally to political ideas about nationalisation of railways or closing the borders to immigrants. It's the discussion in social networks that is the actual mechanism for the acceptance of ideas.

In political organisations (and corporate ones) hierarchical communication is a poor method. You'll rarely adopt an innovation simply because you're told to, unless you're compelled because someone is paying you (e.g. change your work practises), or can put you in jail (e.g. stop drink driving).

The free flow of discussion is essential for people to share their evaluations, and also to adapt or reinvent an innovation. Top down political organisation has very poor sustainability. Almost all innovation come from the bottom up, and it only spreads if there's a strong peer-to-peer network of people with something in common.

by having it adopt new ideas or new ways of working, target the groups in order. Get other Innovators together first. Then focus on persuading the Early Adopters. Then get the Early Adopters to be your human microphone to spread the innovation to the Early Majority. Only then will an idea have the critical mass to become organisation wide.

As socialists, we want to change the way society operates, so innovation is our bread and butter: we have to be good at it. Rogers (and hundreds of other researchers) looked into what factors make an innovation likely to succeed.

Firstly, there has to be a perception that the innovation will be **more efficient** or allow us to **do something new** that we previously couldn't. A mobile phone lets us receive calls away from home; a Labour Party discussion group lets us integrate new Party members.

It has to be **compatible with existing tools** or methods. You might think a new word processor is brilliant, but if you have to change your operating system, you'll probably reject it there and then.

Only a **shallow learning curve** is required to get to grips with it. This becomes more important the further an innovation spreads. Innovators quite like the challenge of figuring out new approaches. Early Majority people want to plug & play. That applies to political organisation or ideas: if you try to explain to the electorate the benefit of Modern Monetary Theory, that requires a lot of background reading on their part before they get the benefit of understanding the idea. Innovations diffuse fastest if there's at least some element of **quick payback**.

Can the innovation be investigated without heavy commitment? If people can see and **evaluate the idea without having to commit** to a lot of time or expense, they'll be easy to persuade.

And perhaps most overlooked: is there a **potential for reinvention**? Do people have to adopt your idea, tool or project on your terms, or can they also apply it to new situations you hadn't considered. If people can innovate with your innovations, it'll probably spread.

An innovation doesn't have to score 10/10 on every criteria for it to diffuse. If the idea is weak in one area, you need to be very strong in others, to ensure take-up will not stall before it gets widely adopted.

Social Conformity

The test of courage comes when we are in the minority. The test of tolerance comes when we are in the majority.

- Ralph Washington Sockman

Social psychology has produced some remarkable experiments that challenge our belief that we are guided by our morality. Most famous is Stanley Milgram's series of electric shock experiments, where under the pretence of a study on improving learning by administering punishments, a naive test subject is asked to shock another person who they believe is also a test subject, when they get questions wrong. It's published in his 1974 book, **Obedience to Authority**.

The pressure to conform to an authority figure in a laboratory setting led 90% of people to give dangerous electric shocks to test subjects, despite their screaming objections. The full length 1962 documentary is available on YouTube, it is worth 45 minutes of your time to watch it[6]. Every subject in the experiment objected at some point, and yet when told to continue, despite the other person screaming to be let free, two-thirds of subjects administered repeated 450 volt shocks to the other person. The shocks were in fact false, but the test was set up so the participants really thought they were giving people electric shocks.

In Milgram's own words, "Ordinary people, simply doing their jobs, and without any particular hostility on their part, can become agents in a terrible destructive process. Moreover, even when the destructive effects of their work become patently clear, and they are asked to carry out actions incompatible with fundamental standards of morality, relatively few people have the resources needed to resist authority."

What is less reported is that Milgram repeated the experiment with an important difference. Five pairs of people (five subjects and five actors) carried out the experiment simultaneously, but all the subjects were in the same lab, and could see each other. This time, once one of the test subjects defied the experimenter and refused to continue, the other test subjects also found the courage to refuse to follow orders. Obedience to authority switched from 90% of people obeying,

[6] Search for: The Milgram Experiment 1962 Full Documentary

despite their protests, to 90% of people disobeying, once someone else had disobeyed first.

A similar phenomenon was investigated by social psychologist Solomon Asch. In his 1955 study he looked at the effect of **group pressure on individual decision making**. A simple experiment was set up where people looked at a reference line on one piece of card, and had to choose which of three lines on another card was the same length as the reference line; this would be repeated with different sets of lines eighteen times. The test was set up so it was quite obvious which was the correct answer, but the real test participant was mixed in with a group of actors without his knowledge.

At first the actors would all give the correct answer, and the test subject, who went last or nearly last, also gave correct answers. Then the actors all started giving deliberately wrong answers. Only 26% of test subjects did not conform and continued to give correct answers, the other 74% were influenced by the group pressure at least some of the time.

Subsequent interviews

GAME OF THRONES

In Game of Thrones, soldier turned priest Brother Ray, played by Ian McShane, speaks about the atrocities he committed.

"I was a soldier once. All my superiors thought I was brave. I wasn't. I mean, I never ran from a fight. Only because I was afraid my friends would see I was afraid. That's all I was, a coward. We followed orders no matter the orders. Burn that village. Fine, I'm your arsonist. Steal that farmer's crops. Good, I'm your thief. Kill those young lads so they won't take up arms against us. I'm your murderer.

...Now, I know I can never bring that lad back. All I can do with time I've got left is bring a little goodness into the world. That's all any of us can do, isn't it? Never too late to stop robbing people, to stop killing people. Start helping people. It's never too late to come back. And it's not about waiting for the gods to answer your prayers. It's not even about the gods. It's about you. Learning you have to answer your prayers yourself."

showed mixed justifications: some admitted they knew it was wrong, but were afraid to speak up. Just as significantly, some test subjects said they were actually influenced by the group, and wondered if their visual judgement had lapsed somehow, and trusted the group over the evidence of their own eyes.

Asch repeated the experiment with different numbers of actors. Having just one person give wrong answers had little effect, but as soon as the subject was in a group of three or more, most people succumbed to group pressure.

In a second experiment, Asch had just one of the actors of a group of seven give the correct answer while the other six actors all gave the same wrong answer. In this case, only 5% of people conformed with the group. Just one other dissenting voice give 95% of the participants the confidence to give the correct answer.

This finding, like Milgram's, highlights the value of even a small dissenting minority. Thinking "this is wrong" doesn't help. You have to stand up and say it. If you do, others will join you.

Both these experiments are in a laboratory context, where there is a very strictly controlled conformist position. Real world political discourse is much more heterogeneous. There are still orthodoxies of common opinion, especially within groups and organisations. If you believe that the consensus is wrong, dissent, ideally before most people have made up their minds. Your dissent will be all the more effective by offering a credible positive alternative. If you can give a cause-and-effect reason, and point towards a positive outcome, you'll take more people with you than if you're simply a naysayer.

How People Learn

I never teach my pupils. I only provide the conditions in which they can learn.

- Albert Einstein

Poverty in 1980's Brazil led many young children to work as street vendors when not at school. Whether they were selling coconuts or chocolate bars, they were all whizzes at mental arithmetic. A team of researchers, Terezinha Nunes, Analucia Dias Schliemann, David William Carraher, investigated where this mental prowess came from. First, posing as customers and observing how the kids calculated prices and gave change, and then later by giving them maths problems in different formats.

They found that the young street vendors had an accuracy of 98% when confronted with a complex problem in an actual transaction - something like "I'll take three coconuts, and four bananas, and pay for it with a 200 cruzeiros note". When kids who'd had typically six years of school were given the same task as word problem in maths, their accuracy fell to 74%. When given the question as numerical symbols, they averaged only 37%, despite six years of formal maths education.

The researchers looked at the process the kids used and concluded that the difference in success was down to meaning. When calculating prices for actual goods in exchange for actual money, they had a clear cognitive impression of what they were doing and why it mattered. Their knowledge and skills were part of a real world activity, and they'd done it many times. The same questions with pencil and paper, which were carefully controlled to be totally accessible to the children's literacy abilities, somehow seemed more abstract, and the kids used slightly different approaches to the problems. When confronted by the standard mathematical symbols, e.g., 4 x 35, the kids defaulted to the arithmetic approach they learned in school, and simply weren't able to instinctively grasp how their calculations related to anything they did in their lives.

In one of the largest data studies ever conducted, educationalist John Hattie correlated surveys of over 500 million children and analysed what actually made a difference to educational outcomes. His conclusions reinforce the findings on the Brazilian street vendors. Of the 195 different approaches, innovations and policies to teaching that he analysed, everything

MARTIAL ARTS

When we founded Talk Socialism we made a conscious decision to use many of the methods we'd developed over the previous decades of teaching jiu jitsu. Not the violent bits, but the fun and learning value of putting people into a situation where they have to figure things out for themselves.

The style of jiu jitsu that we taught was very different from most people's experiences of martial arts. We had no katas, or routine practising of moves in a repetitive way. Instead, we mostly taught through scenarios. For example, students were put in scenarios where they'd be sitting at a table, and another student, acting a part, would walk up, shout abuse, and try to hit them with a (plastic) bottle. Or people would be grabbed from behind; or try to evade two assailants while running for a doorway.

Everything we did had an obvious value, and although there was a lot of detailed support and instruction in individual elements of making it work, it was the freedom to practice the skills in a way that worked for them that make the students so capable.

from wearing school uniforms, variation in class sizes, and classes on study skills, he found that the ones that any real positive benefit were all to do with making the subject more meaningful. These included letting children assess their own work, formative assessments where kids get to interact with teachers when setting curricula, and various forms of questioning why a subject was being taught. In short, getting kids to jump through hoops so we can test them is a waste of their time.

All of this research has focused on childhood classroom education. We all know from personal experience that anything we learn once we're out of formal education is done by interaction. Despite the best efforts of many working in education, governments seem to insist that teachers don't have the freedom to use their judgement and must follow standardised methods, tests and curricula. The traditional classroom model is still based on one person with the knowledge (the expert) broadcasting it to the audience. People are not cars, and education can't be installed on a production line.

When it comes to political education, most organisations seem to unconsciously mimic this approach. We seem to invite a speaker to talk for half an hour, and are pleased when she tells a few jokes to keep our attention. Then a few people ask questions, and most of us go away and forget much of what we've heard. Most panels are the same, but tend to be even drier, where several speakers make the same points. Even many workshops are run on the broadcast-to-audience model.

The research of many other educational psychologists, including Lev Vygotsky, Howard Gardner and Sugata Mitra, has demonstrated that it is only by playing around with what you learn that you actually come to understand it. And you have to play around with it outside of your head. Just as our dreams seem to make sense to us while we're having them, so do our own thoughts seem to make sense to us when we're thinking them. It's only when we have to make something work in the real world, or explain a concept to another person, do we actually have to confront the gaps in our understanding.

We learn by doing. Activity is required. And collaboration, and social mediation, and articulating it to others. In fact, if you can't articulate it to other people, at least in your own terms, you probably can't actually do it. At Talk Socialism workshops we always get participants to come up with solutions to actual problems - anything from persuading a voter to vote Labour (actually an actor), to collaboratively writing down what would be a good defence policy, or even shooting a 1-minute video on their smart phone.

The point is, if political education is going to work, and it has to if we're ever going to get beyond capitalist orthodoxies, we have to make it an active experience where people try out their learning.

Self Determination Theory

The role of a creative leader is not to have all the ideas; it's to create a culture where everyone can have ideas and feel that they're valued.

- Ken Robinson

Have you ever been to a boring meeting? Or maybe turned up to join a group and thought, "this isn't for me"? Or dropped out of a project or cause?

You might have a had a very clear awareness of what wasn't working for you, but in most cases people just get an intuitive feeling that they're just not motivated anymore.

Social psychologists Richard Ryan and Edward Deci put together extensive research on the causes and mechanisms of motivation, which they called **Self-Determination Theory**. Looking at everything from whether people stick to diets to how dedicated they are to learning to play musical instruments, their theory has two main components[7]; firstly identifying levels of motivation and how they manifest, and secondly, looking at what it takes to get people to change from a lower level of motivation to a higher one. At its simplest level, the theory states that unless you can get people to enjoy doing something for its own sake, they just won't turn up. (Unless you pay them).

Which of these do you do: go running to train for a marathon, write poetry, clean the house daily, bake cakes, help at a soup kitchen, enter judo tournaments, organise local political campaigning, go door knocking in council elections, turn up to AGMs of your Labour Party, grow flowers in your garden or windowbox, read philosophy books, attend local fundraisers for a good cause, play in a band, or give talks on local history? If you're reading this, chances are your the sort of person who does at least one of them, but I'd be surprised if anyone does all of them. They will likely appear somewhere on this scale of motivation.

For simplicity, we'll just give the levels numbers:

Level 4: Amotivation (lowest)

Level 3: Extrinsic, External

Level 2: Extrinsic, Internal

Level 1: Intrinsic, Internal (highest)

---

[7] Deci and Ryan's book is over 750 pages long and actually contains 6 mini theories and lots of sub-levels. We've simplified quite a bit. :-)

An activity is **intrinsically** motivated if you do because participation is and end in itself. It's **extrinsically** motivated if you're doing it for the benefits that occur afterwards (or avoidance of penalties, such as having no money or being arrested).

An activity is **internally** motivated if you provide your own motivation - whether joy, or sense of duty, or guilt. It's **externally** motivated if the benefits or penalties come from someone else: payment, praise, promotion, returning a favour.

Level 4 is amotivation. You either have no interest or just can't be bothered, and so you don't do it. For most of us, this applies to most things. Often it's just not on our radar, and we have no real awareness that we're not doing it. But there are also those things that we perhaps see a value in, but we either never seem to get round to doing it, or we just find the idea offputting. For some, exercise fits into this category - they understand the benefits, but the motivation isn't there. For many, political activism falls into the same category. They want the world to be a better place, with less wealth inequality or better environmental outcomes, but for whatever reason they don't actively try to bring that about.

Level 3 is extrinsic external motivation. You do actually get off your backside and do something, at least some of the time, perhaps begrudgingly. For many of us, cleaning the house is like this, or, sadly, going to work in many jobs. We don't do it because we enjoy it, we do it because there's a penalty if we don't, and we want to avoid that penalty. But we tend to just want to get it over with, and our heart isn't in it.

Level 2 is extrinsic, internal motivation. We still don't do the activity because we enjoy it, but out of a sense of self-discipline, or duty, or because we know it's important and don't want to let others down. Many people work diligently at their jobs for this reason; and many people engage in political activism at this level for some of the time. Most of us have probably gone to someone's party or event from a sense of obligation.

LOCUS OF CONTROL & ATTRIBUTIONAL STYLE

Related concepts are locus of control and attributional style. Mostly as a result of lifestyle experiences, some people feel that they are victims of circumstance, and that life is something that happens to them. Others can see the same situation and react differently: they see themselves as agents of change who can influence the outcome, and take control of their lives.

When you see the world is unfair, that the rich and powerful use political influence for their own selfish agenda and cause hardship and blight for millions, you have a choice. You can moan, and complain, and maybe shout at the telly. Or you can find someone who's doing something about it, and join them. It's all a question of how you see yourself.

The main thing we try to achieve with every Talk Socialism workshop is get people to see themselves differently. You can make a difference. Together we are unstoppable.

Level 1 is intrinsic, internal motivation. We do these activities because we actually like doing them. Even if we didn't get paid, we'd still work at these jobs if we could. Even if we don't win, we'd still take part in the sport. Even if we're not published, we'd still write the poetry. Even if there's not an election, we still campaign for socialist ideas.

It should be self-evident by now that activism is only sustainable if you can motivate people to be at level 1. If you're an organiser and get frustrated by people who say they support your cause or organisation, but don't turn up, it's because they're at level 2 or 3. A sense of obligation will only motivate people for a short while. You have to change the experience of the activism to make it enjoyable on its own terms.

Ryan and Deci identified three factors to do this: autonomy, competence and relatedness.

Autonomy is letting people select their own course of action. This isn't a case of simply asking people what they want to do. By all means communicate what's worked in the past, the group norms and traditions, and invite people to take part. It's simply that it must be an uncoerced choice. Volunteers will only come back if they can engage on their terms. Some people hate meetings. Some people don't like social media. Some don't like door knocking. Cajoling people will just make them avoid you. If you want more people to engage, provide more ways to participate.

Competence - no one likes to look foolish[8]. But even when we take embarrassment out of the equation, being unfamiliar with how something is done will cause people to hesitate before initiating actions. If you don't know the procedures or rules of an organisation, you'll be very reluctant to stand for a position. It's deep in human behaviour that we all like to stand back and think we've done a good job. A good grassroots leader will not only thank other activists, but provide a good justification for why their contribution is valuable.

Relatedness is about your emotional interaction the other people involved. Obviously newcomers will not return if people are gruff or rude. But motivation increases massively once we get beyond civil courtesy and start bonding: if you want sustainable activism, you have to have fun, banter, respect for differing abilities, and a lot of personal interaction. The main reason most people don't attend meetings is because there is rarely any warm personal emotional interaction with anyone else there, just polite acknowledgement.

If you want a successful organisation, you need motivated volunteers. Let them engage on their own terms, let them do something they feel good at, and have fun doing it. And don't forget to have fun yourself. :-)

---

[8] Except perhaps clowns, but that's a special case.

Nice Guys Finish First

He who fights with monsters should take care that he does not become a monster, for when you gaze long into the abyss the abyss also gazes back into you.

- Friedrich Nietzsche

You may have heard of the **Prisoner's Dilemma**, a thought experiment from game theory. Imagine two members of a criminal gang have been arrested in a bungled burglary, and are kept in separate cells with no way of communicating. The prosecuting authorities want to charge them with burglary, which gets 3 years in prison. But without testimony from the other prisoner, they only have enough evidence to convict on the charge of forced entry, which gets 1 year. So they offer the prisoners a one-time, take-it-or-leave-it deal: turn informer against the other prisoner, and we'll let you go. She'll get 3 years, and you'll go free. Unless you both turn informer, in which case the court will lower your sentence to 2 years each for cooperating with the authorities.

If you're the prisoner, what's the best strategy? If you keep quiet, you get either 3 years or 1 year. If you give incriminating testimony, you get either 2 years or go free. It's obvious: you should grass on the other criminal.

The Prisoner's Dilemma and other related thought

MAKE FRIENDS

Take principled, uncompromising positions, even if you can't deliver on them. Build up evidence of your opponents' treachery. Brief & leak against them. Get your revenge in first. Outmanoeuvre and out-organise other factions. Make sure your people hold all the key positions, even if they're not that competent. Nice guys finish last. Do all that, and you can be sure of taking over an organisation. You'll also make it utterly useless as a force for socialism, and lose most of your good, honourable, open-minded people along the way.

After one of the Talk Socialism workshops on How the Labour Party Works, where we explain the officer positions, how resolutions are passed, how councillors are selected, etc, a new member approached us and asked, "When I go along to my Labour branch, what should I be aiming to do?" This was just after the acrimonious 2016 Labour Leadership challenge. Jamie and Nick (another Talk Socialism trainer) both simultaneously advised, "Make friends."

experiments, like the **Tragedy of the Commons**[9], are often used as a theoretical justification that socialism is naive. You simply can't rely on people to cooperate for the common good: selfish behaviour always wins out over altruism. That's why markets should be free. Survival of the fittest. Natural selection. Darwinian evolution. Or so it's claimed.

In 1976, evolutionary biologist Richard Dawkins, published The Selfish Gene. Contrary to much subsequent misunderstanding [10], Dawkins provided an incontrovertible argument that although genes are non-sentient, competitive, and behave as if they selfishly maximise their own interests, once you get to the more complex level of human behaviour, this gives rise to cooperation being an evolutionary stable strategy. In other words, we not nice to each other just because we're nice people, it's also the best strategy for all of us in the long run.

This can be represented in a computer simulation. In his 1984 book, The Evolution of Cooperation, political scientist and peace activist Robert Axelrod detailed a computer tournament he set up. He invited entries from across academia to write a computer programme that would play the **Iterated Prisoner's Dilemma** against each other, called the Peace-War game.

In the **Peace-War game** you meet another person (or computer programme) every turn. You can choose to cooperate (work with the other player) or defect (work against them), as can the other person. If you both cooperate, no one wastes resources on competition, and you both get £2. If you both defect, no one wins, and you've wasted energy in the competition, so you both get £1. But if you defect, and your opponent cooperates, you get an easy win and gain £3 and they get nothing. The difference between the standard Prisoner's Dilemma, is you can remember what someone did last time. So people who are cooperators will likely get cooperative behaviour from other cooperators, or may

---

[9] Nothing to do with Parliament. That's more of a farce than a tragedy.

[10] Search online for *Horizon: Nice Guys Finish First*. It's a 45 minute documentary by Dawkins. Well worth watching.

be seen as suckers by aggressive programmes. And those who are constant defectors are likely to get a reputation and never get any cooperative partners.

The surprising result from the tournament, and all of the multitude of re-runs, is that it was won by the simplest programme, called **Tit-for-Tat**. It even beat programmes with complex functions for calculating the probable moves from opponents based on previous decisions. The success of Tit-for-Tat is down to four elements.

1. It is **nice**. With any new partner, it always starts by cooperating. It is never the first to defect.
2. It is **provocable**. If defected against, it will always retaliate. So there's an incentive to keep on its good side.
3. It is **forgiving**. Regardless of the past behaviour, if an opponent cooperates with it, it will immediately make peace and cooperate back.
4. It is **non-envious**. Regardless of how well an opponent may be doing, it still keeps to the simple rule: cooperate-when cooperated-with, defect-when-defected-against.

If a short computer programme can learn the value of cooperation, provocability, forgiveness and non-envious behaviour, we can. In the real world, Tit-for-Tat has the advantage of also being very easy to understand. Everyone who meets you knows what you'll do, and can recognise the value of cooperating with you.

Much of our political endeavour requires us to join large groups, that often have factions or competing cultures and agendas. When we fight internally, we waste most of our energy cancelling each other out. Tit-for-Tat is a simple approach. Even corporate capitalists understand Tit-for-Tat, otherwise there'd be no such thing as price fixing.

It works even better when we move beyond Game Theory and into interpersonal communication. The games assume you have to decide without communicating with the other person. In real life contacts, we often forget that we have the option to communicate outside of official channels.

Cycles of defect-defect occur in organisations when people assume the "other side" are nasty. Often this is nothing to do with genuine disagreements, just differences of micro-culture. How people dress or the formalities and rituals observed at a meeting alert some people to differences, and the assumption that they're opponents who will defect.

Talk to people. Always, always, look for a win-win scenario, and tell people that's what you're doing. Look beyond basic co-existence, and actively say you want to find a positive plan we can all act upon that benefits all parties. Then work collectively to deliver it, which builds mutual trust and understanding. We work together, or we fail apart.

MORE GAME OF THRONES **SPOILER ALERT**

Game of Thrones is notorious for the duplicity, scheming and rivalry between the characters. Yet by far the most politically successful character is not the scheming Cersei, or the honourable and trusting John Snow, but Tyrion Lannister.

Tyrion practises Tit-for-Tat. He's friendly to people when he first meets them. He asks people what they want, and tries to find mutually compatible goals, and goes out of his way to explain that's what he's doing. He asks Bron what he wants, and forges a mutually beneficial friendship with the sell-sword - a mercenary killer. But he's provocable - after Grand Maester Pycelle spies against him, Tyrion has him imprisoned. When Tywin Lannister tries to have him executed, Tyrion escapes from prison and kills him. He's forgiving - in Slavers Bay when Daenerys wants to crucify the masters, burn their fleets, kill every last soldier and raze their cities to the dirt, Tyrion advises killing only the ringleaders and sparing the rest if they cooperate.

Thinking Fast and Slow

This is how philosophers should salute each other: "Take your time".

- Ludwig Wittgenstein

If it takes 5 machines 5 minutes to make 5 widgets, how long would it take 100 machines to make 100 widgets?

90% of university students got this wrong, even though the question was printed clearly. (So if you got it wrong, take comfort in being one of the majority).[11]

The simple correlation between 5 machines, 5 minutes and 5 widgets makes us lazy when we are presented with a question about 100 machines and 100 widgets.

Have you ever had the experience of someone parroting a Daily Mail headline back to you, as if they'd had an insight worthy of Einstein, because it was just referencing commonly repeated phrases?

Psychologist and Nobel prize winning economist Daniel Kahneman explained this in terms of us having two mental systems. **System 1 thinks quickly and intuitively**, and makes its decisions based on familiarity. **System 2 thinks slowly and deliberatively**, and actually stops to analyse information.

This matters because if you're going to have any kind of political involvement at all, you're going to spend a lot of your time disagreeing with people; not just about whether poor people are lazy, but also with your comrades about what tactics or policies your own side should have. And if you're trying to engage someone on the level of system 1, simple intuitive associative thinking, you're going to get high blood pressure. System 1 is not particularly amenable to reasoned argument.

The lesson is, don't write someone off just because they're spouting what to you seems like clichéd platitudes. Give them the chance, and most people will engage in an open minded discussion.

"Labour crashed the economy" is an intuitive, associative, system 1 argument. They must have done - they were in power at the time. Or "we have to win the centre ground" because Tony Blair won a landslide in 1997. Both arguments have an implied

[11] It takes 5 minutes.

conclusion: Labour can't be trusted economically, or socialist policies will be unpopular with the electorate. The problem is compounded, because people accept their system 1 arguments as correct, and then build other conclusions upon them.

System 1 can be right sometimes, too. But only usually where you have a lot of experience and accurate knowledge that you've internalised.

System 2 is deliberative. A quick look at the history of the American sub-prime mortgage scandal will show you that it had nothing to do with the UK government. But you have to check some facts to know that. Or that Labour's 1997 landslide had its cause in the ERM[12] fiasco of John Major's government in 1992, after which Labour was 20 points ahead in the polls, 2 years before Tony Blair became leader. Again, it requires thinking about information that isn't included in the original statement.

System 1 is all about cognitive ease. We're accustomed to thinking that what we're familiar with must be safe, correct or useful. So when we hear things we've heard before, or that are displayed clearly and simply, or even that are told to us with humour or charm, we assume they must be true.

By the way, this applies to you too. Really. We're all subject to cognitive ease. We believe people we trust. Why shouldn't we? The trick is, to separate the argument from the person.

The widget question at the start of this chapter was also shown to other test subjects, but with really poor printing and broken letters. It was difficult to read. Amazingly, only 35% of people got it wrong then. As soon as people have to make an effort to think carefully, they engage their reasoning.

So if you're talking to someone who is unquestioningly accepting a bogus narrative, rather than tell them they're wrong, or making counter arguments, just ask them something that requires some thought. Something simple like, "Does that apply to all countries? I mean, did any other economies crash in 2007?"

---

[12] Exchange Rate Mechanism. Look up Black Wednesday on Wikipedia.

Or, "Are all elections won in the centre ground? Is that what Margaret Thatcher did?" Or even, "But you would agree that it's not as simple as that?"

An additional finding from Kahneman's work is that the confidence we have in our beliefs is a function of the quality of the story we can tell about them. Often, when we're rallying ourselves at meetings or demos, we use simplistic propaganda. If we're to be more confident activists, it would help if we practised making more eloquent and reasoned arguments. We'd then be more persuasive when talking to others. We'd also be more likely to spot flaws in our own reasoning.

A FRAMING EXPERIMENT...

There has been an outbreak of a rare Asian disease.
If nothing is done, 600 people will die.
Two medical treatments are available.

- If treatment A is adopted, 200 people will be saved.
- If treatment B is adopted, there is a one-third probability of saving 600 people, and a two-thirds probability that no people will be saved.

The same scenario was presented to a different cohort, with the questions reframed:

- If treatment A is adopted, 400 people will die.
- If treatment B is adopted, there is a one-third probability that no-one will die, and a two-thirds probability that 600 people will die.

In frame 1, 72% of people chose option A.
In frame 2, 22% of people chose option A.

They are exactly the same mathematically, but how they are framed affects people's choices.

If the scenario outlook is good, people are risk averse, and hold onto what they have.

If the scenario outlook is poor, people are risk seeking, and will take a gamble on a better outcome.

Cognitive Dissonance

A great many people think they are thinking when they are merely rearranging their prejudices.

- William Fitzjames Oldham

In 1957, social psychologist Leon Festinger published his **Theory of Cognitive Dissonance**, describing it as a form of psychological tension.

We all like to believe that our judgement is sound, that we are moral people with good intentions who are justified in our actions and beliefs, and are capable of acting on those beliefs. Most of us are happy to accept that we don't know everything, that we may not be mathematical geniuses, chess prodigies, or gifted musicians; but our confidence depends on us believing we are good judges of character, that we know what's right for us, and we can be trusted (at least according to our own value system).

Then we hit reality, which consistently proves us wrong. We find our judgement is sometimes flawed, that we've acted from motives we are subsequently not proud of, or that we are less capable of changing the world than we thought we were. There's a mismatch (dissonance) between how we think the world behaves and what our senses tell us is happening (our cognition). We experience cognitive dissonance. This is not just disappointment, but the unpleasant truth that we're not as wise or benevolent as we thought we were. It occurs at a subconscious level, as a feeling of unease, rather than a rational evaluation.

If cognitive dissonance gets too high, we become apathetic or even depressed. (There are also many other causes for depression, of course). If we think we might be fundamentally wrong in our judgement, less capable than we thought we were, or start to doubt our own integrity, we become hesitant, indecisive, and fearful of putting ourselves in situations where we might fail. We can become defensive, and angry when challenged on it. If we consider this mental process from a survival point of view, stopping to re-evaluate could be a major evolutionary disadvantage: being hesitant or fearful in the face of an enemy could be disastrous. Better, surely, to be certain but self-deluded than contemplative but dead.

It's important to recognise the difference between cognitive dissonance (the unpleasant feeling), and **cognitive**

dissonance reduction (the process of making that feeling go away).

There are two basic ways to reduce cognitive dissonance. Firstly, you can change your belief, and accept that you were wrong.

This is not easy, however, because many of our beliefs are interconnected and deeply rooted in our sense of self. We often draw much of our self-esteem from our commitment to causes. If a devout Christian comes to decide that his prayers weren't answered because there is no God, it could be a profoundly disorientating experience that cascades through his whole world view, causing him to doubt all his previous choices, beliefs and life decisions, and question all his relationships.

We see similar processes in fanatical football supporters who invest their identity with their team. Admitting your team lost because the other side were just better may be objectively true, but requires admitting you're supporting losers. Much easier to blame the referee, or a fluke deflection.

The second way, which is what most people mean when they say "cognitive dissonance reduction" is to concoct an explanation that explains away our

WHATABOUTERY

One of the most common presentations of cognitive dissonance reduction in a political context is whataboutery.

You'll see it in the comments sections of every newspaper website. When it's pointed out that, say, Conservative politicians have engaged in tax dodging, their supporters cry "but what about all the benefits scroungers who are fiddling the system?"

It's a red herring and a logical fallacy, but the person crying "but what about..." is often unaware of his irrationality. The emotional relief of seeing someone else more deserving of scorn removes the cognitive dissonance, and allows him to settle back into thinking he was right all along.

The simplest counter to whataboutery is not to be drawn by the distraction, and say: "You haven't answered the original point. Are you changing the subject because you don't have an answer?"

misjudgement, so that it doesn't seem like a misjudgement at all. Often it involves blaming other people.

If you're in poorly paid, low skilled work, and have a hard time paying your bills, you might conclude it's because there are too many immigrants. The alternative, that we live in a rigged system that disproportionately allocates wealth to speculators rather than real wealth generators, requires a lot of effort, and also implies you should do something about it. Equally, you could conclude that you're poor because you didn't work hard enough at school, get qualifications, or make the effort to start your own business. Either way, it's much easier to comfort your damaged ego by blaming immigrants.

On a personal level we make excuses for our behaviour. If we've treated someone in a way that we would not like to be treated ourselves, we conclude that they provoked us, or they were asking for it, or that it was necessary to get the job done. The alternative is to admit that we got caught up in our own perspective and let our emotions get the better of us; although that may be good for long term personal growth, it can be exhausting in the short term. Evolution has not prepared us to be good at long term thinking; it mostly prepared us to survive until the next crisis.

People can also avoid situations that create cognitive dissonance. A major reason why people don't do the things in life they know, logically, are necessary, is because it requires confronting the unpleasant fact that hard work is needed. Far easier to stay a bit flabby than experience the discomfort of exercise, or just to watch TV box sets rather than become politically active and do something about the social and economic injustice that you know is wrong.

We are all subject to cognitive dissonance, because we are all human and fallible. But we have a choice about how we deal with it. We can choose excuses and blame, and faith in some kind of greater power, whether that's a supernatural deity, the self-emancipation of the working classes, or that next week I really will win the lottery.

Or we can constantly allow for our misjudgements, accept mistakes are inevitable and that we should learn from them, and put the effort in to raise our game in all our endeavours. The best defence against self-delusion is good friends who will tell you the truth as they see it, and making sure you accept constructive criticism with good grace.

Wisdom of Crowds

This is not the wisdom of the crowd, but the wisdom of someone in the crowd. It's not that the network itself is smart; it's that the individuals get smarter because they're connected to the network.

- Steven Johnson

In 1906, statistician and polymath Francis Galton[13] observed a "guess the weight of an ox" contest at a farmers' fair in Plymouth. 787 entrants saw the live ox and guessed its weight after it was slaughtered and dressed. Afterwards, Galton obtained their entries and calculated the average; although individual entries varied considerably, the mean guess was 1,197lbs, only 1lb from the actual true value. So, using this and many other examples, the concept of the **wisdom of crowds** was born: the idea that the average opinion of a large group is more accurate than any of the members within it. In 2016 a man of much lesser intellectual capacity than Francis Galton, Michael Gove, suggested we "have had enough of experts".

It's statistics, really. The more measurements you take, the less reliant you become on the erroneous ones. Plus, at the farmers' fair, they all knew what an ox was and could see it.

But why do large groups often get it spectacularly wrong? What about stock market crashes, or cases of mass hysteria like the Salem Witch trials or mass fainting epidemics? A Swiss research team asked two groups to estimate the length of the Swiss-Italian border. One group made their guesses independently; the other was asked to discuss their answers before making individual guesses. They found that the more that people had discussed it, the less accurate the answer became as people began to conform to a group norm. We all see this phenomenon in the Westminster Bubble of political journalism.

In his 2004 book, The Wisdom of Crowds, James Surowiecki identifies four elements needed for effective crowd decision making.

1. **A diversity of opinion**. Crowds that think the same rarely outperform the individuals within it in terms of accuracy.

---

[13] Cousin of Charles Darwin, Galton invented the weather map, made strides in psychology, and even wrote articles on the optimal method of making tea and cutting round cakes without radial incisions to stop them drying out for 3 days.

2. **Independence**. That people's opinions aren't determined by the opinions of those around them.

3. **Decentralisation**. People are able to draw on their own, specialised knowledge rather than a central source.

4. **Aggregation**. There has to be a mechanism to bring together all the collective estimates and average them in some way.

The problem with the wisdom of crowds is it only really works for simple questions with numerical answers. It's good for simple predictions, but what about more creative or conceptual tasks? In 1999, via the Internet, Garry Kasparov played the Rest of the World at chess, including teams who had computers to help them. Kasparov won, not least because he was able to consider a longer term strategy and had a unity of purpose that the Rest of the World team lacked, because it voted for its moves on a daily basis.

If in 1950 there had been a competition in The Times to write in and describe the molecular structure of genetic building blocks, it's hard to imagine that the most popular answer would have been a double-helix DNA molecule. Some questions need a sound understanding of the concepts involved. In the Kasparov chess game, 2.7% of people voted for moves that were illegal - they didn't even understand the rules.

This has a bearing on how groups reach decisions, including policy positions. Complex decisions require an understanding of the questions involved, otherwise people tend to change the question to one of popularity, and end up electing Donald Trump.

For the group to come up with a better decision than its brightest members, it requires lots of opinions where information can be shared, but draws on diverse experiences of people who at least understand their own area of competence.

If we're going to have good policies on constitutional reform or economic policy, we need an educated populace. The diversity of experience and aggregation of differing values requires that people can at least speak a common conceptual language. Very few people can explain a concept like monetary policy, and so have nothing useful to add when considering whether the national debt justifies cutting public expenditure or raising taxes. In the end it gets left to committees of experts who don't have diverse opinions, mostly being educated in similar schools of thinking, and whose discussion tend to aggregate to a consensus rather than bringing together diverse opinions. Even if we assume the goodwill of the participants, a homogenous group like a cabinet of millionaires, most of whom attended exclusive public schools, will miss something that might be blindingly obvious to someone who gets by on minimum wage.

Better political decision making requires more people who at least know the basics. Set up reading groups, and pitch them at an introductory level. Make videos explaining the ideas in nuts-and-bolts terminology. Avoid fixed policy positions based on majority voting from delegates - open up discussions to conferences and seminars. Discuss ideas from new sources,

NETWORKED EXPERTISE

A camel is a horse designed by a committee. Whether it's how to democratise nationalised industries, or the structure for a progressive movement, there's undoubtedly a need for a democratic but focused decision system.

Techniques known as Networked Expertise, the Delphi Method & Dialectical Bootstrapping are all variations on a theme. People who are knowledgeable, at least in part of the subject, ask questions of relevance, and propose ideas. An independent facilitator (or team) aggregates these and distributes them, ideally anonymously. All participants are active in the process, and read the ideas, and are allowed to combine, mix and adopt them, and then the process is repeated. This cross fertilisation of ideas combines specialist knowledge and the benefits of diversity and independent thinking. Rather than a board with X delegates from here, and Y delegates from there, and a token Z delegate, all voting on the resolutions or policy documents, you get a proper development of ideas.

especially ones you disagree with. Many groups have political or economic gurus whose work attains the status of scripture, and becomes equally ossified.

The same applies to political strategy - how to build groups and win campaigns. Most of the best decisions are the result of people stating ideas, others commenting on them, getting critical opinion from knowledgeable people outside the group, and then having an informed consensus that remains responsive to change as new information comes to light.

Philosophy

Learn one way; react.

Learn many ways; understand.

- Tadeu Dias

Philosophy is probably the most misunderstood field in the humanities. Over the past two and a half thousand years philosophers have been keen to assert their opinions on every subject under the Sun, and all those above it too. It's not surprising that the general population think philosophy is about old Greek blokes deciding they must exist because they think they do while simultaneously wondering whether trees that fall over make a noise if there's no one there to hear it.

Philosophy frames our thoughts. It is essential because it frames our thoughts, whether we realise it or not.

Our critical thinking skills are our philosophical beliefs being applied in practice. You have only to ask someone which way they will vote - and why - to reveal a whole substructure of underlying assumptions about the way the world works, how they evaluate whether an argument is sound, the way they view evidence, whether ideology is more important than material comfort, and their views on free will and incentives.

For many people, their philosophy is quite rough-hewn. People who've never even heard of Immanuel Kant or Ludwig Wittgenstein have a good working grasp of whether to trust someone and how they think people should treat each other. It is when you move into questions outside their personal experience that people quickly become hesitant and inconsistent. Without a framework of established ideas, it's hard to decide what is possible and what makes sense.

Understanding it is not really a question of intelligence, it's mostly a question of experience and training. It may be the case that to make breakthroughs in philosophy you need a good dollop of natural talent. But to reach a robust understanding of critical thinking needs nothing more than an open mind and the curiosity to learn. That said, open minds are not as common as we might wish.

Philosophy has a knack of asking questions about the assumptions that people take for granted. You might have heard a politician talking about the school curriculum, and how we need schools to have greater rigour and testing in order to prepare our children for tomorrow's job market. If you ask "why is that the purpose of education, rather than developing well informed, civic minded adults?" you've asked a philosophical question. You have shifted the frame of the debate.

So rather than tearing your hair out at the idiocy of people who can't seem to grasp basic concepts of fairness, for example, you might find a quick tour of some philosophical ideas could help you cut through all the tangled undergrowth that keeps people believing the status quo is the only way things can work.

It is the mark of an educated mind to be able to entertain a thought without accepting it.

Cultural Hegemony

A man will be imprisoned in a room with a door that's unlocked and opens inwards, as long as it does not occur to him to pull rather than push it.

- Ludwig Wittgenstein

How do you know what you take for granted? Does the Earth revolve around the Sun, or does the Sun revolve around the Earth?

The philosopher Ludwig Wittgenstein is once reputed to have spoken to a student who said, "The reason people thought the Sun revolved around the Earth is because it looks like the Sun revolves around the Earth." "What," Wittgenstein replied, "would it look like if the Earth revolved around the Sun?" The answer, of course, is exactly the same. The difference is in the preconceptions.

If you're a medieval peasant, you probably don't care very much either way. If you were told by your 14th century priest that the world is at the centre, a quick glance in the sky with provide you with confirmation. Likewise, if you grew up in the 20th century, when you see the Sun travel across the sky, it confirms what you learned as a child: it's the rotation of the Earth.

When we hear claims in political discourse, we typically evaluate them by comparing them, often subconsciously, with the implicit theories we believe. For most people these theories are unexamined, and taken for granted because everyone else seems to take them for granted. That's what's known as a hegemonic idea. Once a hegemonic idea takes hold, like all theories, people moderate their perceptions to fit the theory, and tend to ignore data that doesn't fit.

Hegemony is rooted in social status. Whatever is seen as being of high status often comes to be regarded as the right way to think and behave. It's easy to see examples of people who have gained success and who work hard, and to see people who are not achieving highly and do not work very hard. So, the dominant ideology is reinforced. But it's even easier, if you just look, to see people who work their socks off and are still amongst the poorest in any society: cleaners, labourers, care workers, low paid workers in general. The hegemonic idea, though, kicks in, and people think, "Well, maybe they should have tried harder at school. Gone to night school, even."

People tend to fit the examples to the assumed idea that everyone has got what they deserve, and anyone can be what they want, if only they try. That's why, of course, the royal family are so rich, because of all their hard work after being born into poverty. The Tory cabinet likewise; they all invested their paper-round money to get where they are; none of them made contacts at the exclusive public schools they attended. But challenge this idea, and it's the politics of envy.

It's reinforced with glossy magazines, programmes about £200,000 cars, celebrity gossip. That's what you're supposed to want. From school onwards, where it is casually and subtly said many times every week of a child's life, that the important thing is to pass your exams and get a good job. Don't be like one of those poor losers. Why could it not be said that your objective is to become a caring person with healthy relationships with your family and friends? Nope; the game is indoctrinated from childhood: you're an economic unit competing with everyone else. Hegemony is about consent. It's about values becoming so pervasive that people accept that it's a law of nature.

Don't despair, though; we humans are also very good at recognising when we've been swindled. Once ideas of solidarity and co-operative work are presented to people, they see the idea

ORIGINS OF HEGEMONY

Originally, hegemony referred to political, economic and military influence by a strong power. For example, the British merchants in the 19th century very rarely had to deploy the country's military might to protect their trade advantages; the very knowledge that Britain had that power was usually enough to secure compliance. Mix in some diplomacy, threats and local bribery, and the ruled often accepted the rulers as inevitable, and took the path of least resistance. Later, the concept was extended to cultural hegemony, particularly by writers such as Antonio Gramsci. The basic idea is that the status quo becomes "common sense", whether because "things have always been that way", or "there's no alternative", or it's some expression of natural law or justice.

has a much better fit with the world they observe. Any theory that has better explanatory power becomes the dominant one over time; the challenge is to get the ideas out there for people to think about. We spend so much time fire-fighting on specific campaigns and defending hard-won rights that we forget to articulate the overarching idea that humans are inherently co-operative, that we are more creative when we are secure, and that selfish competition is wasteful.

It doesn't require us to all go and get PhDs in philosophy and economics; the ideas are not unduly complex. It does require us to fight and engage on the level of ideas, and not of personalities; it requires us to engage and win on the level of ideas and not of causes or emotions or tribal loyalties. We have to be able to clearly and concisely say why state investment in public services is not just nicer than the free market, but actually more effective too. We have to be able to articulate why laissez faire capitalism isn't about rewarding innovation, but encourages monopolies, tax-dodging and asset stripping. We have to be able to give examples about why people aren't inherently selfish, but inherently co-operative and also inherently motivated to gain social status and respect. Above all, we need to be able to narrate that there was a time before capitalism, and there will be a time after capitalism. Another world is possible.

Zeno's Paradox

I think we ought always to entertain our opinions with some measure of doubt. I shouldn't wish people to dogmatically believe any philosophy, not even mine.

- Bertrand Russell

In the 5th century BCE the philosopher Zeno of Elea proved that it is impossible to overtake a tortoise. The argument runs something like this:

The swift footed Achilles has a race with a tortoise, and gives it a head start. In order to overtake the tortoise, Achilles must first draw level, since it is impossible to be both in front of the tortoise and behind it at the same time. But by the time Achilles gets to where the tortoise is now, it will have moved. So now, Achilles must draw level to the tortoise's new position. Again, though, by the time he gets there, the tortoise will have moved. So now he has to draw level to the new position, but when he gets there, the tortoise has moved again, and so it goes on forever. Achilles will never catch up with the tortoise.

Zeno's point wasn't that it's impossible for Achilles to overtake a tortoise. It's blindingly obvious that you can, both by observation, and by any of a host of other logical arguments. His point was that if you can use logic to prove it is impossible, then there must be something wrong with the framework of our logic. The philosophers of his day had views about the nature of motion that he wanted to challenge. I'd like to think that Zeno chose the example of Achilles and a tortoise because it was so obviously untrue, and so very easy to disprove in practice, that it illustrated his point all the more clearly.

Today, we have people who think that because an argument is logical, it must be true. They come up with self-contained theories that seem to make sense, but have never been tested in practice. We hear these all the time in fields of human behaviour, both from know-it-all drunks in the pub, know-it-all columnists in the newspapers, and know-it-all economists who come up with theories like trickle down. If you want to solve poverty, you need to give people an incentive to work, so cut their welfare. Since businesses pay tax, then all wealth must come from the private sector in order to fund the public sector. Just like Zeno, they have started with a point they want to make, and then invented an argument to prove themselves right. The difference

LOGICAL FALLACIES

A related form of argument is the straw man, which uses an argument that superficially sounds like your opponent's, but smuggles in some different assumptions. You then proceed to show that the original argument results in something ridiculous, and rely on the audience not noticing that the argument doesn't actually apply to your opponent's original position. As socialists, we're often characterised as wanting to take wealth from people who work hard and give it to people who don't. That's actually capitalism.

is, Zeno was clever enough to know he was creating a paradox to prove a philosophical point.

Our know-it-alls invariably make an assumption that appears sensible, but actually only holds true under certain conditions, then proceed extrapolate as if their assumption was a universal law. I can jog up my 3-metre flight of stairs in 3 seconds. Mt Everest is 8,848 metres high, therefore I can jog up it in 8,848 seconds - about two and a half hours.

Zeno's is the first known example of what is called **reductio ad absurdum**, where you take someone's logic, extend it, and show that it results in absurdities.

What's this got to do with socialists? It's a lesson to check our thinking. We're proposing changing the way we organise our societies and economies. It would be wise to check that our thinking isn't based on unchecked assumption or logical fallacies.

Incidentally, Zeno was involved in a revolution to overthrow the tyrant Nearchus, and was captured and tortured. With his dying breath, he told the tyrant to lean in close, and he would reveal the names of his co-conspirators. When Nearchus leaned in close, Zeno bit his ear and did not leave go until he was dead. Philosophers can be fighters too.

There is actually a philosophical answer to Zeno's paradox, but that's for another time. If you want to know, you can catch up with us at one of the Talk Socialism sessions.

Rhetoric

Speeches are like babies – easy to conceive but hard to deliver.

- Pat O'Malley

Some arguments are more persuasive than others - even when making the same underlying point. Rhetoric is often used as a by-word for spin or flimflam, but it's actually the study of effective communication. It can help us answer the question: why are some arguments more persuasive than others?

There have been many models proposed over the centuries, but one of the simplest and most useful goes back to the ancient Greek philosopher Aristotle.

He proposed that arguments can be of three basic appeals: ethos, pathos or logos[14].

Ethos is an appeal to trust. You should accept my argument because I am a trustworthy speaker. That might be because I am an expert in the field, or because I have practical experience. We're more likely to believe a doctor's opinion of the NHS than a rocket scientist's. Trust can also be gained by having things in common with the audience, or at least appearing to. Nigel Farage (a commodities trader) and Donald Trump (a property billionaire) both pretended to "speak it like it is" and be anti-establishment, man-of-the-people types.

Ulterior motives destroy ethos. We all assume, without any verification, that an independent witness is more reliable than the person on trial. Likewise in political discussions, if someone says "you're just saying that because you want my vote," it would be foolish to deny it; a better answer would be "I do want your vote, but that's not why I'm saying it. I'm saying it because I believe it's true."

Pathos is an appeal to emotion; the English words sympathy and empathy derive from pathos. You should accept my argument because its outcome is about fairness, justice or the ending of suffering. When the Independent published the picture of 3-year old Alan Kurdi whose body washed up on a Turkish beach, it turned the public opinion regarding refugees.

---

[14] Not to be confused with Athos, Porthos and Aramis (The Three Musketeers)

That so many people are dependent on foodbanks, or that corporations and wealthy individuals dodge paying their taxes are also arguments based on ending suffering and unfairness. Equally, though, arguments about benefit scroungers lazing around living of hard-working people's taxes are also appeals to emotion.

Logos is an appeal to logic, using a simple cause and effect argument. It's largely based on assumptions people have or will accept, but that they've not previously connected. The issue of national debt has been a front-line topic since the financial crash. Logically, some argue, we have to cut public spending in order to repay the debt. It's a simple, self-contained argument. It's also wrong. Logically, if you're in debt, the best course is to earn more money; cutting expenditure caused further economic slowdown and instability, which is why every debt-reduction target was missed.

The appeal to logic is limited by the understanding your audience has of the subject. If, after you've said it, they can't see the cause and effect relationship, your argument will have little effect. Explaining the benefit of the Keynesian Multiplier to someone who doesn't yet know how tax is collected will be futile; as author Robert Heinlein said, "Never try to teach a pig to sing. It wastes your time and irritates the pig."

The value of this model is that it's simple and self-evident. All three modes of argument are useful, but in general, listen to what your interlocutor is saying, and respond with an argument of the same form. Socialists often default to pathos; we talk about how unfair it is that public servants have had their pay frozen, but if the person you're talking to is concerned about the national debt being unsustainable, you will have little persuasive effect, even if they agree that the pay freeze is harsh. You have to talk to people on their terms, not yours.

The Ten Second Rule.

Aristotle also spoke of **kairos**, or timing. It's natural to assume that if you give people more information, your argument will be more persuasive. It's not true, though. People make up their minds based on your opening statements. Conversations come in many kinds, and ten seconds is not a hard and fast rule. But you have to get to the point quickly, and make your argument self-contained, or based on knowledge your interlocutor already has.

You might want to explain the ills of the global financial system in detail, but one short, simple example will probably be more effective.

In Talk Socialism workshops we practice the **Ten Second Rule**. If you can't make a persuasive point in ten seconds, go away and practice until you can. That's typically about 30 to 40 words. If you do your job well, your first ten second argument will persuade a person to listen to your next ten seconds. And who knows, you might also give them time to share something useful with you.

BREVITY IS THE SOUL OF WIT

A key feature of good communication is that it's short.

Explanatory Power

Any scientist who can't explain to an eight-year-old what he is doing is a charlatan

- Kurt Vonnegut

How do we know if a socialist economy will work? It's a valid question, and there is no short answer that is conclusive. Equally, how do we know if a free market economy will work? If you're living in a slum in Mogadishu, or sleeping on the streets of London, the claims of capitalism's prosperity will ring hollow. Even the answer, "let's try it and find out" won't be conclusive - we can't run a controlled experiment and see what the world would have been like if we had taken a different course.

This problem is not unique to politics and economics. Even in a subject as precise and testable as physics, different theories need to be evaluated against each other, and evidence interpreted in accordance with the theory. At school you probably learned some Newtonian Physics (though you may not remember it), and that if you apply a force to an object, it will accelerate in proportion to that force (F=ma). Then Einstein came along with his Theories of Relativity and demonstrated that Newton was wrong about that; as you get faster, the relationship no longer holds true. In fact, you can't get beyond the speed of light.

But does that mean Newton was wrong? If you subscribe to the Instrumentalist school of thought, you'd say no. Newton's theory was just incomplete. Context is key. If you're interested in calculating the airspeed velocity of an unladen swallow, Sir Isaac's theories will do the job very nicely indeed, and with much less effort than Dr Einstein's. **Instrumentalism** argues that theories are just tools - instruments - not philosophical statements of absolute truth. The whole point of a theory is that it's useful, and if it reliably allows us to calculate an outcome, then it's true in that context.

No theory is ever likely to be final, independent of all context, and able to predict everything in detail. Economics and politics are not natural sciences; running replicable experiments is simply not possible. But if we're going to argue for wholesale reorganisation of taxation, public ownership of key industries, and changes to the money supply, we should at least have a solid framework of how we will evaluate our progress.

FALLACY OF COMPOSITION

The Fallacy of Composition is the logical error that if something is true for part of something, it is true for the whole of that thing. If one unemployed person tries incredibly hard to find a job, he will probably succeed. Therefore, all that is required to end unemployment is for the unemployed to try harder!

Sadly, no. It's a zero-sum game: the only thing that changes is who gets the jobs, not the total number of jobs available.

The question then is not "is this theory correct?" but "is this theory better than the alternative?" Most of what is taught in economics courses has no bearing on real world policy questions, and has zero correlation with what happens in the world.

Neoliberal and neoclassical economics says that we should interfere as little as possible in the markets, and strip away regulation. Modern Monetary Theorists say we should create money via central banks to provide meaningful employment until we're close to full employment.

We can evaluate these competing theories by borrowing from the philosophy of science. The concept of **Explanatory Power** gives criteria by which we should prefer one theory to another. We should prefer one theory if:

1. It accounts for more facts or observations.
2. It changes more surprising facts into matter of course. Events that seemed out of the blue are actually simply explained in the model.
3. It is highly accurate and precise.
4. It makes accurate predictions, and not just explanations of the past.
5. It depends on many more observations, and isn't just based on a few examples.
6. It makes fewer assumptions. (Ockham's Razor)
7. It is more falsifiable.
8. It is hard to vary.

Most people intuitively get points 1 to 5, that you evaluate the strength of a theory by its accuracy and weight of evidence. Points 6 to 8 require a bit more thinking.

William of Ockham, a 13th century monk, coined **Ockham's Razor**: the explanation requiring the fewest assumptions is most likely to be correct. If you need lots of untested assumptions to make your theory make sense, it's probably a poor theory. There's a good chance that those assumptions might not hold true in many real-world situations. Neoclassical economics in particular is riddled with unfounded assumptions about how people behave, and falls prey to the fallacy of composition.

Philosopher Karl Popper developed the concept of **falsifiability** in 1934. While thinking about the difference between Einstein's Relativity and Freud's psychology, he noticed that there was no new piece of information that could, even hypothetically, prove Freud wrong. With Einstein, his theory would be proven wrong if we could observe light passing close to a massive object like a star, and it did not bend. His theory would be contradicted by evidence. But when you tell a Freudian that, no, really, I don't want to sleep with my mother, he can say, "Ah! So you're in denial!" Politics and economics is replete with unfalsifiable theories - little more than idealistic fancies that the world works in this or that way.

David Deutsche, in a 2009 TED Talk[15], adds the final criterion: a good theory has to have a good explanation that cannot be easily changed if new evidence comes along. "Whenever you're told that some existing statistical trend will continue, but you aren't given a **hard to vary** account of what causes that trend, you're being told a wizard did it." In other words, just because two things happen at the same time doesn't mean that one causes the other[16].

---

[15] A new way to explain explanation. YouTube it.

[16] Like the rise in global temperatures being caused by the reduction in the number of pirates (look up Flying Spaghetti Monster).

How can we Justify our Values?

Integrity is telling myself the truth. And honesty is telling the truth to other people.

- Spencer Johnson

Moral philosopher Phillipa Foot posed the **Trolley Problem**:

Suppose there is a runaway train with no one on it heading down the tracks. There are five workers, who will have no chance to get out of the way and who will certainly be killed. However, although you're too far away to warn them, you are next to a lever to switch the points and divert the train into a siding, where it will kill one person. You can either:

a) Do nothing, and the train kills five people on the main track, or

b) Pull the lever, divert the train, and one person dies.

Which is the most ethical choice?

This is less abstract than it might sound. We might soon have driverless cars: how should we programme them to respond to situations like this?

In surveys, roughly 90% of people say they would switch the points, justifying their choice by saying it's better to save 5 lives than 1 life. They are taking a **consequentialist** approach to morality, that the morality of an act is defined by its consequences. A sub-category of this is **utilitarianism**, which says that morality is defined by achieving the most good for the most people. The idea has been around as long as philosophy, but was developed and refined by Jeremy Bentham and John Stuart Mill (a very early campaigner for women's equality).

Utilitarianism is used to justify many socialist policies: we should redistribute wealth from billionaires, who would barely notice the loss of a few million, to make a huge difference to the lives of those in poverty.

But suppose we look at drunk driving. If you drink five pints of beer and manage to drive home without an accident, have you done anything immoral? Or if you try to assassinate a rival by poisoning her coffee, but by chance she doesn't drink it. Those acts had no harmful consequences, but we irk at the idea that they are not immoral.

HUME'S GUILLOTINE

Hume's guillotine is named after 18th century philosopher David Hume, who pointed out that any attempt to justify a moral position (we ought to...) cannot depend on an observation (what is).

Land mines kill or maim around 15,000 people each year (an "is"). Therefore we should ban them (an "ought"). There is in fact no logical justification for linking them except for our personal moral choice. If you think the profits of arms dealers are more important than those people's lives, then you will conclude that we ought not to ban them.

In the end, you have to choose, and accept moral responsibility for your politics.

Rule based utilitarianism is distinguished from **act based utilitarianism** by considering what would typically happen if the actions were repeated by many people over time. Clearly, if people frequently drive drunk or poison people's coffee, it will result in injuries and death. This provides us with a more general moral framework that we can use, especially in situations where exact outcomes are hard to predict on a case by case basis.

But (as you've probably anticipated) this can run into problems too. Consider the **Transplant Problem**, attributed to Judith Jarvis Thomson.

A surgeon has five patients each in need of a different organ, who will each die without that organ. There are no organs available. A healthy traveller, just passing through the city the doctor works in, comes in for a routine check-up. The doctor discovers that his organs are compatible with all five of his dying patients. Suppose further that if the man were to disappear, no one would suspect the doctor. Do you support the morality of the doctor to kill that tourist and provide his healthy organs to those five dying persons and save their lives?

The numbers are the same as the Trolley Problem: 1 person dies to save 5. But most of us find this viscerally immoral, regardless of consequences.

Deontology, (from the Greek *Deon*, meaning *rule*) says that we should derive our morality not from its consequences, but based on inviolable principles of right and wrong. As Captain Picard says in Star Trek, "I refuse to let arithmetic decide questions like that!"

Deontology is wide field, covering everything from inalienable human rights to religious commandments. One person might regard freedom of sexuality as a moral principle, another might condemn homosexuality as a Biblical abomination. Neither is arguing from a logical position, but a foundational belief.

Virtue ethics, by contrast says that morality consists of doing what a good, upstanding person would do. Along with deontology, though, it is heavily based on cultural expectations. In samurai Japan, a good upstanding person might, from kindness, kill a rape victim to prevent her suffering shame. We would be horrified by such behaviour.

Pragmatic ethics takes the position that we're culturally evolving, and not always for the better. Like science, our current beliefs may be supplanted in future, so for now we may practise another form of ethics, but we should endeavour to research and examine our morality, and prioritise education and open public discussion, and not make morality a matter of dogma and pejorative judgement.

Evolution vs Revolution

I kept the faith and I kept voting

Not for the iron fist but for the helping hand

For theirs is a land with a wall around it

And mine is a faith in my fellow man

- Billy Bragg

Revolutions happen all the time. The industrial revolution. The Internet revolution. The sexual revolution in the '60s. Political revolutions where one government ousts another. In Britain, there have been many revolutions: in 43 CE the Romans invaded; in 410 they left; from 793 Vikings invaded, in 1066 William the Conqueror lived up to his name and overthrew the existing social and economic elite and replaced them[17]. Cromwell and other revolutionaries took power by force in the 1640s; the Glorious Revolution of 1688 put the Dutch William III in charge. The 1918 Representation of the People Act gave the vote to 8.4 million women and extra 5.6 million men.

Karl Marx & his best bud Frederick Engels acknowledged there were many forms of change, but said the one that really mattered was about who gets to control society's economic power. They called for a proletarian revolution, where the mass of ordinary workers would **seize the means of production**, and determine for themselves what should be produced and how it should be distributed.

There have been many attempts at class-based revolutions, the two most successful, at least in terms of overthrowing a wealthy ruling class, were the French Revolution of 1789 and the Russian Revolutions of 1917. But none of those overthrew a modern market economy; they overthrew despotic monarchies, and soon returned to despotism. The question of how you would overthrow a representative democracy, and what you would replace it with, is not a question that was on the table when Marx was alive. Indeed, should we even be thinking in terms of "overthrowing"?

It's unfair to categorise all revolutionaries as thinking like the People's Front of Judea: "Right. Now, uh, item four: attainment of world supremacy within the next five years." (But there are a few like that[18].)

---

[17] He was also called William the Bastard. He lived up to both names.

[18] Splitters!

NO BLUEPRINTS?

In 1848 Marx and Engels proposed 10 policies in the Communist Manifesto, including some that look remarkably mainstream today: progressive income tax, free state education for children, and nationalised canals, roads and railways.

In the preface to the 1872 version, they state that the policies of socialist society would "depend on the historical conditions existing at the time" - fair enough, as a general point. Today, though, some self-identifying revolutionaries extend this, and decline to offer a vision of what a socialist society might be like, citing "there is no blueprint for socialism" and it will be "up to the workers to decide".

Frankly, this is a cop-out. If you want people to join your cause, you have to tell them what it means in practice. You can put caveats in, people know things will change over time, but without outline policies for what it would mean to daily life, why should people follow your lead? And what if you win some power - you'll need some provisional plans ready. Socialists should be in the business of looking at policy and drawing it up - always reserving the freedom to revise it and improve it.

The vital question is: who gets to make the decisions? The question of power, both political and economic, is central to socialism. Often governments look very different, but don't upset anything significant in the distribution of power and wealth in society. The 1945 Labour government was an exception; it really did make massive changes in a short period of time, many of which have endured despite constant political attack.

Identity politics misses this: "we need more women as CEOs of major corporations" is not a socialist policy; "we want fewer people of any gender being exploited in insecure work" is. Of course, you can't have true economic freedom without gender and racial equality, and removing other barriers to freedom. We're using that example to show that there's nothing inherently egalitarian about having power concentrated in a woman's hands instead of a man's: Margaret Thatcher, anyone?

At what point does a stream become a river? At what point does a society with progressive taxation, a free NHS, education and living pensions and participatory democracy become a socialist country?

There is no "**final crisis of capitalism**" and there is no "arrived at socialism". Socialism, like capitalism, is a word that's a proxy for a whole raft of legal, cultural, philosophical and economic behaviours in a society. You can't simply aim to take power, and then deliver socialism.

A socialist society requires changes to the way we educate children and adults, the way we relate to each other, the way we think about what our life goals should be, and the way we think about individual responsibility.

It will require huge numbers of people to realise that they have both the power and the responsibility to make the world a better place for them and those they care about. Above all, it requires a rethinking about the relationship between individuals and the state. Marx knew that; many who follow him missed that. There is no lever in No 10 Downing Street that we can set to "socialism".

The question for socialists should always be:

a) if you had power, what would you do to make things better, and

b) what can you do, now, to bring about that change anyway?

The process of social transformation is huge and many faceted; writers like Noam Chomsky, Michel Foucault and Antonio Gramsci have described the relationship between knowledge, ideas and power. We won't change power relationships by having lists of radical demands and protesting against sitting governments. Any lasting change has to built on a foundation of changing the way people see themselves. Radical, small-scale changes to the status quo don't look revolutionary, but they change both people's immediate reality, and the way they see the broader reality of society.

PHILOSOPHY: EVOLUTION VS REVOLUTION

Evolution and revolution are part of the same process; it's a false dichotomy; all socialists want to change some things forever, and all want to keep some things the same. Just as with the origin of species, evolution is a continuous stream of small revolutions, and the occasional mass extinction event. The mass extinctions are dangerous and unpredictable for all involved.

As a start, we take power over our own lives and communities in small ways, and we should do it with people's consent. It's a contagious approach that will grow.

On the Spectrum

Although it is not true that all Conservatives are stupid people, it is true that most stupid people are conservative.

- John Stuart Mill

Who is more religious, a nun who works in a missionary hospital in Africa, or an ISIL fighter in Syria?

It's a stupid question in many ways, both are clearly highly motivated by their ideological framework. But there can be no meaningful comparison, because religiousness is not a quality that can be measured by any units, or where one person's quantity can be compared against another's.

This is why talk of hard-left or soft-left is not only pretty meaningless, but actually damaging to constructive debate, and encourages a lot of straw-man arguments. It's little more than labelling people as belonging to different tribes, and inhibits productive discussion about some important political questions.

You might have seen some Internet quizzes that plot your views on two dimensions, known as a **Nolan Chart**. Personal views are plotted on one axis - attitudes to crime, drugs, relationships; and economic views on the other - attitudes to wealth distribution, taxation, etc. That's an improvement over the "spectrum", but realistically we have to think beyond models we can draw on a flat surface. The people who advocate freedom of sexuality correlate poorly with the people who advocate the freedom to own firearms. What about vegetarians: are they liberal, or authoritarian[19]?

Ideally, we would want to have a coherent political philosophy that is consistent, supported by evidence, and chimes with our moral values. For now, though, we'll start by looking at four political dimensions relevant to socialist activism, and leave you to find a mathematician to construct a tesseract to plot them on.

Authoritarian vs libertarian

This covers issues of personal freedom and the rights of the state to interfere with individuals, such as drug laws and the age of sexual consent. Over recent centuries the West has moved to greater individual liberty, and universal human rights are

[19] Goldwin's law says that in an argument, the first person to make a comparison to Hitler loses.

accepted by many. Issues like state surveillance, though, and detention without trial, proved very divisive under Tony Blair's Labour government. Some questions, such as the right to assisted death or abortion, or the freedom of parents to choose a child's religion, or circumcise their children, still run into conflict: whose freedoms do we prioritise: doctor or patient, parent or child?

Hierarchical pyramids vs distributed networks

This is more to do with our view of what is efficient than what is moral. The question of how we should organise decision making is becoming increasingly salient with the ease of modern communications. Traditionally, organisations of the state, private industry, and the Labour movement mirrored each other in being an organisational pyramid. There were huge differences, of course; an army officer could have a private up on a charge, a shop steward can't. But all hierarchies concentrate knowledge and decision making, and therefore power, into appointed specialists. The Marxist-Leninist version of socialism calls for a centrally planned economy, a very hierarchical approach.

Modern organisational research tends to favour distributed decision making as much as possible. Many capitalist corporations work in this way, with self-managed teams. Most professionals in the public services - teachers, doctors, probation officers, argue that they should be allowed to get on with their jobs and use their own judgement rather than being told what to do by central government.

Egalitarian vs elitist

Pretty much everyone who self-identifies as a socialist would claim to be egalitarian in the sense of believing we all have equal rights. But that quickly runs up against practical questions. Should we let everybody take turns at chairing a meeting, or should be have a system that chooses the most competent person for the job? Do you really believe that everyone's opinion is equally valid? What's your view on intelligence: are some people just cleverer than others? Should the activists in a movement have more influence over decision making, by means of turning up to more meetings, or should everyone get a vote in online

OMOV[20]? Should we trust an MP's judgement on who should be leader more than an ordinary member's?

The more elitist you are, the more you tend to subscribe to the view that people have to earn their influence, whether by skill, experience or diligence. The more egalitarian, the more you think that everyone should have an equal say, regardless of their abilities or actions.

Pragmatic vs idealistic

How should we evaluate the merit of political ideas, plans and policies? When we are forced to choose, should we pursue a course that brings some likely gains at the expense of compromising some of our values, or should we stick to our values and sacrifice some gains? Compromised victory or glorious defeat? Note, we said "forced to choose". The New Labour myth that we must abandon socialist ideas or abandon the hope of electoral victory was pure poppycock with zero explanatory power.

But the question was a real one for the 1945 Labour government, when the BMA (British Medical Association - then substantially politically different from now) threatened to derail the NHS. Nye Bevan famously said he "stuffed their mouths with gold" (many of the concessions were actually about clinical freedom and doctors' rights to self-organise).

Given that the structure of an organisation affects the group dynamic - whether it's a political party or workplace - our attitudes to these questions can have a significant impact on what we do and our collective success. Whether we're hard-left or soft-left is ambiguous and vapid; what freedoms people should have and how we think we should organise is important.

[20] One member one vote

Economics

When I give food to the poor, they call me a saint. When I ask why the poor have no food, they call me a communist.

- Helder Camara

"The purpose of studying economics is not to acquire a set of ready-made answers to economic questions, but to learn how to avoid being deceived by economists." So said Joan Robinson, Professor of Economics at Cambridge University.

Whenever a socialist policy is suggested, the primary objection you hear from interviewers, newspapers and Tory politicians is that economic reality won't allow it. We hear claims like "the private sector creates the wealth that the public sector spends", "competition is good, which is why we have to have an internal market inside the NHS", "if you try to regulate the market, the bankers will just leave the country[21]", and most recently, "if you put taxes up, you'll actually collect less tax". Every one of these claims is based on absolutely no evidence. It's scarcely different from the priests of ancient Rome looking at entrails of birds and saying, "Don't anger the gods!"

The mainstream of economics is the **Neoclassical** school, which is what is exclusively taught in most university economics courses. Contrasted with it are a host of **Heterodox** economic schools, **Keynesian**, **Post-Keynesian**, **Marxist**, **Austrian**, **Institutional**, **Modern Monetary Theorist**, and others, which can often disagree with each other totally, and have radically different political positions.

In fact, the meaning of the word economics depends upon your school of thought. Economist Karl Polanyi used the term **substantivism**. He pointed out there are two broad views of what economics means - the insubstantial version defined by neoclassical economists refer to economics as the study of laws and relationships between peoples actions and the distribution of scarce resources. Pretty much everyone else takes the substantive view, and thinks economics is about something real and practical: how people make a living, interacting with their social and natural environment.

Mainstream economics is divided into two fields.

---

[21] To which the correct answer is: "Good. I'll offer to drive them to the airport myself."

Microeconomics looks at the principles by which individual consumers and businesses interact. It tries to establish foundational laws like supply and demand, the efficiency of markets, and how people make decisions about consumption and expenditure. Most of it is speculation, and there are many fundamental principles which have been contradicted by observed evidence. In particular, Neoclassical economics assumes all economic actors make rational choices, and then goes on to define rational choices as those choices that the actor made: they must have been rational, or they wouldn't have made them. It make Alice in Wonderland look sensible.

Psychologists who examine economic decision making, like Daniel Kahneman and Dan Ariely have contributed to the field of **Behavioural Economics**, which undermines most of the claims of microeconomics.

A great place to read more is Steve Keen's **Debunking Economics**. It's not a beginner level text, but is much more accessible than most economics text books.

Macroeconomics, the branch that looks at the workings of an economy as a whole, tackles the causes and policy options for addressing taxation, inflation, unemployment, economic growth, interest rates, free trade practises, and questions of national debt. Although there are lots of theories, and many attempts at mathematical formulae, the field is largely based around correlations of statistics. Its predictive power is about as accurate as a compass in a magnet shop.

The primary failure of neoclassical economics is that it tries to extrapolate from microeconomics into macroeconomics. We used the example earlier: I can jog up my 3 metre high staircase in 3 seconds, therefore I can jog up Mount Everest, at 8848m in 8848 seconds, or 2.5 hours. No. You cannot simply assume a mathematical relationship will hold true far beyond the point where it was originally observed. You have to find evidence that it works in that context.

A word of caution, though. Although economics is not the science that many mainstream economists claim it is, it is not simply speculation either. Although there is no comprehensive theory of economics that is remotely scientifically accurate, headway has been made on many individual policy areas, and many causal relationships have been shown to be reliable. In particular, although economics often can't provide reliable methods for working out answers, it does provide a conceptual framework for thinking about them. It won't do to advocate replacing capitalism if you have no idea how wealth is produced, for example, or the relationship between banks and money.

A great place to start is with Ha-Joon Chang's **23 Things They Don't Tell You About Capitalism**, perhaps followed by his **Economics, The User's Guide**. Although he's an eminent economist, Chang's books are explicitly written for those with no prior knowledge, and his style is very accessible. We set up a reading group, and run through them one chapter a month. It's a great way to start a political education programme and allows people to make the connections between economic theory and its real world impact on their political lives. Get in touch if you want some advice about setting up your own group.

Perhaps the most important thing to remember about economics is that it is a value-laden subject. At the level of public policy, all economic decisions are political decisions.

All Production is a Social Enterprise

Before you finish eating breakfast in the morning, you've depended on more than half the world.

- Martin Luther King Jr

Leon, Jamie's 9 year old son at the time, was doing maths question at home, and said, "Dad, I have a problem with this question."

The question was from an American maths book: *From her diner, Katherine earns $400,000 each year before taxes. The federal income tax, state income tax, property taxes, licenses, payroll taxes take two-fifths of her money. How much of her money does she pay the government each year?*

Jamie was quite surprised: "Really? That's just a simple percentage question." (Leon is very good at maths).

Leon: "No, it's that she's earning $400,000 a year and she's objecting to paying taxes. If there was no tax, there'd be no road coming up to her diner, so she wouldn't have any customers, or be able to get any deliveries. And there'd be no police to stop her getting robbed."

It was a very 'proud father' moment.

In his Christmas Sermon on Peace, where the breakfast quote comes from, Martin Luther King was talking about the international interconnectedness of production. Production is also intricately interconnected though time and across professions. As Leon realised, none of us ever produces anything without the help of others. We hear right-wing ideologues claiming that the government is taking "their" money, or Margaret Thatcher prattling: "The problem with socialism is that eventually you run out of other people's money." But it was never their money in the first place. Just like Katherine's diner, the only way anybody makes any money is in conjunction with other people, most of whom they have never met.

Dr King wasn't exaggerating when he said "half the world." The effort into making a cup of coffee goes beyond who grew the beans. Those beans had to get here. Someone had to make the ship and the lorry. You had to heat the water, maybe using an electric kettle. Who generated the electricity? Who designed the power station to make that electricity? Which primary teacher taught the midwife to read, who grew up to deliver the engineer who designed the power station? Who were the firefighters who kept that school safe?

Once you begin to trace the whole cumulative effort that goes into even the simplest act of production, you quickly realise that anyone who makes a profit at anything only does so by the implicit cooperation of everyone else.

People who object to paying taxes from "their" money need to be reminded it was never their money in the first place. Not paying tax is theft, pure and simple.

SOCIAL CONTRACT

"There is nobody in this country who got rich on their own. Nobody. You built a factory out there - good for you. But I want to be clear. You moved your goods to market on roads the rest of us paid for. You hired workers the rest of us paid to educate. You were safe in your factory because of police forces and fire forces that the rest of us paid for. You didn't have to worry that marauding bands would come and seize everything at your factory... Now look. You built a factory and it turned into something terrific or a great idea - God bless! Keep a hunk of it. But part of the underlying social contract is you take a hunk of that and pay forward for the next kid who comes along."

- Elizabeth Warren

What is Wealth?

It is we who ploughed the prairies, build the cities where they trade

Dug the mines and build the workshops, endless miles of railroad laid

Now we stand outcast and starving midst the wonders we have made

But the union makes us strong

- Ralph Chaplin

ECONOMICS: WHAT IS WEATLH?

The most common and damaging error in economics is the assumption that money is the same thing as wealth.

Socialists the world over are asked, "where will the money come from?" Or "who will pay for it?", usually with a smug sneer as if the questioner thinks himself practical and worldly.

The fact is, money is utterly useless except as a means of persuading other people to do things. The money isn't the wealth. This isn't even a particularly socialist concept in economics; theorists from across the political divide agree that the money is just a token of exchange. It's quite obvious, really. Having a wad of banknotes, or more likely a number in a bank's database, has absolutely no practical value whatsoever, unless other people choose to accept it as currency.

Consider a thought experiment: go to Mexico, or France, with £10,000 in British ten pound notes. Try and rent a car, or pay for your meal with it. You can't.

But surely there is some connection between money and wealth? After all, people will go to great lengths to get money, including doing dangerous and unpleasant work, or risky criminal acts. True; but only because they believe implicitly that other people will accept the money. In previous eras, people would go on crusades to redeem their souls: motivation comes from belief. Beliefs we accept without question are very powerful.

Real wealth is people doing useful things for other people. Cutting your hair, manufacturing your car, teaching your kids, purifying your water supply, putting on a play, catching the criminals who want to break into your house. In any complex economy you can't expect this to be done on the basis of reciprocal trust, so we have socially evolved the collective idea that we will use money. But the money is just the means of persuasion. The problem is that it is entirely possible (but not easy) to get lots of money while doing absolutely nothing whatsoever to generate wealth.

The limits on real wealth are real people, their knowledge and skills. Imagine it's 1920, and you have a billion dollars. You

RENT SEEKING

This fact was acknowledged long before we had our modern economies: David Ricardo, at the time of the Napoleonic Wars, railed against "rent seeking" capitalists who basically just collected rent off the land they had inherited, while adding nothing whatsoever to its value, in contrast to the entrepreneurial capitalists whom he favoured, who at least put the work and innovation into organising production.

Today, rent-seeking (or rentier) is out of control. Investment bankers literally make up things to bet on, called derivatives, like whether the price of oil will rise, or whether a housing scheme will go bankrupt. They then trade these bets using the savings people have put in their bank accounts, and take out huge commissions, which they spend on yachts, cocaine and penthouse apartments. The whole process contributes literally nothing of value whatsoever. A single shelf stacker contributes more to real wealth.

get an infection, and want a cure. All your money won't help, because no one has invented antibiotics yet, and your doctor can only ease your pain; you still die. A generation later, those antibiotics would cost pennies, and any pharmacist could help.

Wealth isn't just a function of scientific advancement either. Try another thought experiment: you have to survive on an isolated tropical island for a year, and can take two people with you. Who would be more use: a professor of theoretical physics, or a gamekeeper? An airline pilot, or a gardener? (It's a generalisation, of course, the professor could have grown up on a farm and be a very practical person[22].)

The collective limits on wealth are in fact the ability to efficiently deploy the skills of the people. A more skilled workforce means a wealthier country. More people working close to their potential means a wealthier country.

When we have graduates working in call centres

[22] Or perhaps you like the idea of being alone on a tropical island with Professor Brian Cox.

or making coffee because that's all the work they can find, our combined wealth is being wasted. When we have small businesses struggling with obsolete equipment because they don't have access to investment funds, potential wealth is being wasted. Where we have millions of people working in jobs below their potential because they can't afford the training they need, we are squandering human talent. When we have millions struggling with mental health and alienation, we are wasting the creativity and energy that could enrich us all. Money is just an implied agreement - it has no value outside of our acceptance of it - it need not and should not be a barrier to economic development.

In short, if we want to be wealthy, we have to direct the money away from sitting idly in the bank accounts of the rich, and into funding small businesses and training ordinary people to work in fulfilling jobs they find motivating.

Where Does Money Come From?

Money has no essence. It's not "really" anything; therefore, its nature has always been and presumably always will be a matter of political contention.

- David Graeber

For most of us, money appears in our bank accounts as a result someone else paying it in. We might draw some of it out in cash machines, but most of our transactions never see a piece of paper; your rent or mortgage, utility bills, council tax, grocery shopping, almost all of them are paid electronically by direct debit or using a bank card. Which raises the question, where is this money, and how real is it?

In 2017 the UK has £73bn in circulating currency[23], - notes and coins, including the pristine wads of notes stored in bank vaults and the tarnished pennies down the back of your sofa. That's called the **narrow money** supply, or in economist speak, the M0 money supply. The Bank of England prints the notes, on polymer these days rather than paper, and sells them at face value to companies in the Note Circulation Scheme. These organisations (G4S, RBS, Post Office, Barclays & HSBC) put them in cash machines or sell them on to other organisations. This raises a question, though: if you want to buy Sterling banknotes, what do you use to pay for them? The answer is electronic money.

The total **broad money** supply in 2017 is £2,700bn. This includes the cash, and all the 'money' in bank accounts, technically called the M4 money supply. So only £73bn out of £2,700bn is cash. The rest, 97.3% of it, is electronic money. So where does the electronic money come from, and what form does it take?

Private banks create electronic money by typing it into a spreadsheet. Seriously - this isn't a lefty-conspiracy theory. The **Bank of England**'s own report states: "Whenever a bank makes a loan, it simultaneously creates a matching deposit in the borrower's bank account, thereby creating new money.[24]" Which means that 97% of money is created by private banks.

It works something like this. You decide you want to buy a house, and somehow have scraped together the deposit. You go along to Barclays, say, and try to borrow £200,000. They have a

---

[23] The money supply figures in this chapter are from the Bank of England

[24] They've even made a video. Search YouTube for: Money creation in the modern economy

look at your credit rating, and the computer says "yes". What they then do is create £200,000 in your bank account. Just like that. They simply create it, by typing the numbers into a computer, and their database now says you've got an extra £200,000. Of course, there are certain regulations about fraud and money laundering, but now there's an extra £200,000 in the economy that did not exist previously.

The common myth is that banks lend out money that other people have saved with them. Once upon a time this was true - when gold was money. Because only a few people would withdraw their money at any one time, they could lend out much more than was deposited. It's called **Fractional Reserve Banking**. But that has not been the case for decades.

So how much money can banks create? The short answer is as much as they can get away with, because they are interconnected through the interbank transfer system. At the end of each day, all the banks total up how much their customers have spent with each other, and arrive at a net figure. Suppose in total all of Barclays' customers have spent £500mn with Nat West customers, and Nat West customers have spent only £450mn with Barclays customers. So Barclays owe Nat West £50mn. To make these transactions balance, Barclays transfer £50mn of **central bank reserves** to Nat West.

Central bank reserves are electronic money, created by the Bank of England, and only used by banks to make payments between each other. They are effectively the special bank accounts that only banks can have, that are operated by the Bank of England. It really is little more than a spreadsheet. Banks that are lending too much, and receiving not enough back, will find their central bank reserves depleted, and need to borrow from another bank. If other banks say no, the bank collapses, as happened to Northern Rock in 2007. Or the government can bail them out with money that it either creates or borrows.

The interest you earn on bank savings is also connected to this system because your bank's central bank reserves earn interest. For every £1 Barclays has in the central bank reserve, the

Bank of England adds the appropriate interest, also created electronically. In effect, the Bank of England sets the bar for interest charged on borrowing and on savings.

If Barclays offers its customers appealing interest rates on their savings, sooner or later their customers will deposit money spent by customers of other banks, and their central bank reserves will increase. If they'd get more interest on their reserves than they have agreed to pay to their customers, their reserves increase. So in practice, commercial banks set interest rates on savings below the BoE base rate, and charge borrowers more than base rate.

The implication of all this, is that money is literally created at the stroke of a keyboard. We can never run out. As long as people have confidence in it, a government can do what it wants with money. People think money is like gold: there's only so much to go round. That's not even true of gold, by the way: we keep mining more all the time.

If you want to know more, check out **Positive Money**'s excellent video series.

QUANTITATIVE EASING

Quantitative Easing is where central banks, like the Bank of England, create extra electronic money and uses it to buy financial assets held by private companies, like banks and pension funds. Since 2009, the BoE has created £445bn in money, mostly used to buy government bonds (i.e. government debt).

This meant that those private financial institutions swapped bonds for cash, which in theory would be lent out to stimulate economic growth.

In practice, 92% of the cash flowed into financial assets, like property portfolios and shares, boosting their prices by around 20%. If you had a million quid in financial assets, you got a £200k windfall. If you're poor and own no shares, you got zilch.

There is absolutely no economic reason why QE could not be used to do something useful instead - like fund a **National Investment Bank**, to make sure money does go to small businesses, and the development of publicly owned assets like green energy and up to date transport infrastructure.

Keynesian Multiplier

A more productive economy in the long term will bring us higher tax revenues, but that requires long-term investment in infrastructure and the skills necessary to grow a balanced economy.

- Jeremy Corbyn

What happens to money when you spend it? As a private citizen, it's gone, somewhere else into the economy, and you get your goods or services in return. You seem to have used it up, and have to wait until pay day for some more.

But think about it on a system-wide level. The money isn't destroyed when it's spent, it just changes hands. One person's spending is another person's income. So every time we spend money, someone else earns money. And in the grand scheme of things, these all go round in a big cycle. Just like when it rains, the clouds haven't destroyed the water. They've just moved it: it flows into streams and rivers, reaches the oceans, evaporates and becomes clouds again.

Spending money doesn't use up money, it just moves it. The most common effect of spending money is to motivate someone to do some useful work: bake your bread, deliver your groceries from the factory to the supermarket, generate your electricity, produce your favourite TV shows. Eventually it goes full circle: when they spend money, all those people indirectly pay you to do your job (if you have one). John Maynard Keynes described this effect in the context of government spending, called the **Keynesian Multiplier**.

Much of the press would have you believe that government spending causes the country to lose money. But even a moment's thought shows that what it does is transfer money from the government to private hands, whether as the wages of public sector staff, or the turnover of private businesses. What do they then do with it? Mostly, spend it.

Let's look at an example. Suppose the government hires an extra firefighter on £30,000 a year, that's £2500 per month. Where does that money go? Every month £500 (approx) goes straight back to the treasury in income tax and NI. So already, an extra £2500 a month in public spending only costs £2000.

The rest of the £2000 per month goes where? A bit might be saved, but in practice, UK savings for the non-rich are close to zero. Some goes into a pension fund, which is invested by fund

DYSFUNCTIONAL RICH

If rich people spent their cash by sponsoring artists to create new works and funding scientists to develop new technologies, then wealth inequality wouldn't be nearly the problem it is. In real life, though, the rich sit on their money and don't spend it in the real economy, just on property and asset speculation. So money is not being used for the one thing it's good for: making people do productive work. When poor people or those on median incomes get money they spend it pretty much straight away, creating demand for goods and services, and providing reasons to innovate. It's not envy that causes us to object to billionaires, it's that the rich are economically dysfunctional. They impoverish us all.

managers, largely by lending it back to government in the form of bond purchases.

Most of the rest is spent in the local economy. If he goes for a night out to a gig at a local pub followed by a meal, 20% of that goes straight back to the government as VAT. The rest goes to paying the wages of the bar staff, restaurant staff, local performers, etc., all of whom in turn pay tax, buy things that have VAT on them, and so on. Some goes into the local business owners' profits, who, like the staff, spend it.

In total, the entire £30,000 of government spending ends up either creating employment, taxed in sales and income taxes, saved or invested.

But not just once: all of the money spent in employment goes round several times; by spending the money, our hypothetical firefighter's salary has ended up in the pockets of bar staff, chefs, small business owners, and probably plumbers, mechanics, and shop workers too. All of whom are then able to spend a little bit more than they otherwise would, and all of whom pay a little more tax than they would, and as a result more people are employed or given more hours of work.

This process continues over time, and the money continues to circulate in the economy (until the investment bankers crash it, anyway). So by spending £30,000 hiring a firefighter, not only are we all kept safer, we are all made richer - a bit.

By how much? That depends on how much under-employment there is. Where business is booming and pretty much everyone who wants a job has one, at their full skill level (rather than graduates making coffee in Starbucks or working in unpaid internships) then extra spending won't create more employment, because there are no more people to employ - so it just puts up prices. But when employment is slack, and businesses aren't investing or increasing capacity, the effects can be huge.

There are many different ways of measuring the multiplier effects, depending on how far into the future you measure the data. But as a rule of thumb, when there's slack in the economy, the multiplier is between 2 and 2.5. That means every £1 of government spending grows the economy permanently by £2 for every year thereafter. In times of deep austerity, like the years since 2010, one IMF report suggested the multiplier is as high as 6![25].

But why does it need the government to do this? Why doesn't the money go round on its own? In short, because the money gets stuck like a logjam. If things are left to the market, individual businesses don't have an incentive to invest unless they are pretty certain they'll make a good profit back, and reasonably quickly. Remember that in free market capitalism, the only objective a business has is to maximise its profits, rather than to work for the good of society.

So we get a situation where spending slows down. Businesses ease back on investment, and freeze hiring because it looks less profitable. Aggregate demand across the economy slows down because earnings have fallen, and businesses are not spending on investment, so buy less from each other. The cycles cascades across the economy - causing more investment and recruitment freezes. If governments cut spending at these times,

---

[25] That's an exclamation mark. Not 6 factorial.

it cascades further, making the situation worse. The multiplier can be negative as well as positive.

You cannot cut your way out of an economic recession. You can only grow your way out of it.

MMT and Fiat Currency

Our banking system grew by accident, and wherever something happens by accident, it becomes a religion

- Walter Bigelow Wriston (US Banker)

I promise to pay the bearer on demand, the sum of ten pounds. So it says on every ten pound note.

It's a common misconception that you can go into a bank, or at least the Bank of England, and ask to exchange your tenner for £10 worth of gold. You can't. As the Bank of England says on its own website, "Public trust in the pound is now maintained by the operation of monetary policy, the objective of which is price stability."

Since the end of the Bretton Woods agreement in 1971, most currencies, including UK Sterling, have been **Fiat money**. The currency has no real, intrinsic value, except that a government says it has. The thing about governments is, though, they have a lot of force to back up their claims, so everyone accepts it. In the case of fiat currency it is taxation that makes us use it.

You could come to a deal with your boss that you'll be paid in Tesco vouchers, if you wanted, but when you have to pay your car tax, the government will only accept payment in Sterling, and can crush your car if you don't. It'll also lock your boss up if he tries to pay your PAYE and NI contributions in Tesco vouchers. Thus, the government automatically creates a demand for its own currency.

For this reason, it can never, ever, run out of money to buy things in its own currency. It can always issue more. Excessive over issuing can eventually lead to inflation if it is not spent on productive projects like improving infrastructure, health or education, or if you already have full employment. But it is more than a generation since Britain had anything like full employment.

The fact that Greece did not have its own fiat currency, but had the Euro, which is controlled by the European Central Bank, is why they were forced to accept austerity. In the UK, austerity is a political choice, it's not an economic necessity.

We've seen that private banks create money every day[26], and the government can create money whenever it wants via

[26] See the chapter: Where does money come from?

Quantitative Easing or similar methods. So why can't the government spend what is needed to provide good public services and full employment?

The short answer is that it can if it wants to. It would upset some investment bankers, who do very nicely out of the current arrangement, but the objections are political not economic. Financial institutions have a lot of lobbying power.

The term **Modern Monetary Theory**, or **MMT** was coined by economist Bill Mitchell[27]. It contains several components, developed since the 1990's by many economists, including Hyman Minsky and Randall Wray.

MMT is not a policy, it's an economic theory that explains how money works in the 21st Century. What it does is explain the likely effects of certain government policies that a country with a fiat currency might plausibly do. As Bill Mitchell says,

"When a Conservative politician or corporate leader claims that the government has run out of money and therefore cannot afford income support for

SECTORAL BALANCES

If we look at an economy as a whole, one person's spending must be another person's income, and one person's debt must be another person's credit.

Economist Wynne Godley introduced the concept of sectoral balances, the idea that if the government is in debt, then the private sector must be in credit. And if the government runs a surplus, then the private sector must be getting into debt.

In the UK, and most of the western world, governments and households are heavily in debt. The corporations, especially the financial institutions, are strongly in credit.

Incidentally, Wynne Godley predicted in the early 70's that unemployment in Britain would reach 3 million in the 80's. In 1992, Hyman Minsky predicted a massive banking collapse would occur in the 2000's. Steve Keen predicted the 2007 sub-prime mortgage crash with pinpoint precision. These MMTers have a pretty good track record.

---

[27] He's got a very well indexed blog

the unemployed any longer at the levels previously enjoyed, MMT alerts us to the fact that this is a lie and that there must be an alternative agenda."

So why can't we, as a country, just buy everything we want right now?

Because it hasn't been built yet. As we said in the chapter on What's Wealth, no matter how much money you've got, you can't buy something that doesn't exist. Money is a way of persuading people to do things. But no amount of persuasion can enable me to successfully do something that is physically impossible.

The real constraints to a zero-carbon energy generation system, for example, are not the lack of money, but the lack of skilled project managers, engineers and technicians, and manufacturing facilities. MMT isn't a policy, but it allows us to pursue policies of sustainable, long term investment. The constraints on everything from zero carbon energy, excellent mental health care, free university education, and free nationwide broadband wifi are skills, technology and organisation. Money is not the constraint.

In 2004, the M4, broad money supply[28] was £1,190bn. 5 years later, even before the quantitative easing programme began, the broad money supply was £2,190bn. Private banks created £1000 billion in five years. Since then £445bn has been created in Quantitative Easing to stabilise irresponsible financial institutions.

As soon as we realise that a government with a fiat currency can choose to fund whatever it wants to, we can focus our collective efforts on building a better society.

---

[28] See the chapter: Where does money come from?

Bubbles and Crashes

Corporation (noun): An ingenious device for obtaining individual profit without individual responsibility.

- Ambrose Bierce

The orthodoxy of classical and neoclassical economics, from Adam Smith onwards, is that economies are self-correcting. Sure, they go through business cycles, but they always tend towards equilibrium, with markets efficiently allocating resources, and unemployment tending towards zero. The problem with this idea is that it's absolute ivory tower claptrap: the simplest glance at history proves it wrong in all places at all times.

Neoclassical economist Jean-Baptiste Say said in 1803 that the economy was essentially a bartering system, so stability was inevitable if only governments would leave well enough alone. Real economics was trading good for good, money was just a lubricant, allowing a wider trade network. In 1949 Arthur Pigou published the Veil of Money; "Money is a veil behind which the action of real economic forces is concealed."

Keynes disagreed, saying that money allows transactions to occur over time, and that financial markets influence production of real goods and services.

In 1992 economist Hyman Minsky published the **Financial Instability Hypothesis,** which was a culmination of work he'd published since the 1970's. Money, he claimed, was no longer a veil that hides the real workings of the economy: it has become the economy. He opposed the deregulation of the 1980's, and predicted that money would less and less represent real wealth. The banking system no longer matched lenders to borrowers; "innovations" such as CDOs and CDSs would cause runaway financial speculation and destabilise an economy with debt.

In the 1970's, **Collateralised Debt Obligations**, (CDOs) were invented, where a host of individual debts are packaged by a lender, some high-risk, some low-risk, and sold off in chunks to another institution, most likely in the shadow banking system. In theory, CDOs are very safe, because although the chance of any one borrower defaulting might be unpredictable, by packaging loads of debts together, the odds of simultaneous default by lots of borrowers was effectively zero. Or so they thought.

A **shadow bank** is a financial institution that engages in trading, creating financial products, borrowing and lending on an investment scale, but does not operate a normal deposit system. As such they are not part of the central bank clearing system, don't have a central bank reserve account, and not subject to the same levels of regulation. You trade with them at your own risk.

In 1994, **Credit Default Swaps** (CDSs) were created to allow shadow banks to bet on the rising or falling prices of debts, ostensibly as a form of insurance. A fund could, in theory, take out a CDS against any CDO, and pays a regular premium, and if a price falls to a certain level, it receives a payment. So if you own loads of CDOs, and they went down in value, you'd offset your losses. In practice, though, these were virtually unregulated and were bought and sold as speculative instruments by people who didn't even own any CDOs.

Minsky's hypothesis described three types of borrowers.

Hedge Borrowers, who can afford to pay the interest on a loan, and in time repay the principal, from their current income.

Speculative Borrowers, assume that the good times will continue to roll. They know that at present they can only afford the interest on a loan, but assume that their income will rise, and eventually they'll be able to pay off the principal amount too.

Ponzi Borrowers can't afford to even make all the current interest payments. But because the value of the asset they are buying keeps rising in value, that's okay (they reason). The $100k house I bought today will be worth $150 next year, and I'll borrow against the increased asset value to pay the 10k interest, and make $40k profit.

However, house prices only continue to rise faster if more people are trying to buy them with an expanding money supply. Banks, and particularly bank traders, encouraged this behaviour, because they made massive bonuses. Northern Rock famously lent people 125% mortgages: they could borrow without any deposit and get an extra 25% of the house price. Eventually, though, you have to lend to riskier and riskier borrowers, who default. Unsold houses appear, and the market stalls, and prices stop rising. All the Ponzi buyers can no longer borrow against a

BREAKING UP THE BANKS

After the 1929 Wall Street crash, a series of laws were introduced in the US called the Glass-Steagall Acts. They made it illegal for a commercial bank to engage in investment banking. Commercial banking includes current accounts, normal business accounts, and mortgage lending. Trading in financial assets is investment banking.

The 1929 crash had been so damaging because the banks were a labyrinthine mess of interconnectedness, and investment banking divisions dragged down the commercial arms of the same banks.

In 1999, the Gramm-Leach-Bliley Act repealed it. Commercial banks could get in on the high-risk, high-reward world of CDOs and CDSs.

In the UK, in 1986 the Thatcher government introduced two laws. The Building Societies Act allowed the traditional mortgage lenders to legally become banks, and engage in financial speculation. The Financial Services Act of 1986 deregulated derivatives from oversight by the courts, allowing untrammelled casino capitalism.

In 2008 we were told the banks were too big to fail, so we had to bail them out.

rising asset price. All the CDOs and CDSs create chaos, as the feeble regulation means no one knows exactly who owns which debt.

Thus was the financial crash of 2007, which has subsequently been used to justify the cut-price sale of Royal Mail, a 14% wage cut for public servants, the tripling of student tuition fees, the rise of food banks, proliferation of insecure work and zero-hours contracts, and the Bedroom Tax. If left unregulated, the economy clearly does not tend towards equilibrium.

We strongly recommend watching a couple of films: **Margin Call**, with Kevin Spacey and Jeremy Irons is a brilliantly acted portrayal of the unfolding of the crash from inside a merchant bank; and **The Big Short** is a highly entertaining film that does a great job of explaining the entire sub-prime crisis from the perspective of shadow bank traders who stumble upon the insanity of the system.

Inflation and Hyper-inflation

Rising prices or wages do not cause inflation; they only report it.

- Walter Bigelow Wriston

Inflation is the rate at which prices are going up. In the UK, it's calculated by the Office of National Statistics, using surveys of approximately 6000 people every month. The idea is to be able to work out how much prices have changed over time. They produce an aggregate statistic called the **Consumer Prices Index**, or CPI, which is intended to represent the increase in the cost of living year on year.

An inherent problem in calculating inflation is that we simply don't buy the same things over time, because the same things often don't exist. How much was the monthly broadband Internet fee in 1980, or a Netflix subscription? Likewise, some things massively fall in price because of changes in productivity and technology. In 1993, an IBM 386 computer cost approximately £1500, today you can buy something ten times the power for a quarter of the money, even before adjusting for inflation. So inevitably, statisticians have to make opinion-based judgements about what contributes to the cost of living. It's not perfect, but it is at least based on real, accurate data.

So what causes prices to rise?

According to classical, neoclassical and monetarist economists from Adam Smith onwards[29], stated that the price of goods was directly proportional to the amount of money in existence, called the **Quantity Theory of Money**. The basic idea is: if all of the nation's assets can be represented by ten apples, and we have ten gold coins, then the price of an apple is one gold coin. If we create ten more gold coins, as actually happened after the conquest of the Americas, then there are now ten apples but twenty coins, so each apple costs 2 coins.

The full theory also considers the **velocity of money**, i.e. how quickly it changes hands; you can check it out on Wikipedia.

To be fair to Smith and co, money has significantly changed in the intervening centuries, and a strong statistical evidence base did not exist then. The monetarists of the late 20th

[29] Even Nicolaus Copernicus, the 15th century astronomer, advocated the theory.

century have no such excuse. Money now has nothing whatsoever to do with gold.

The quantity theory of money is hegemonic, but it's false. We've even heard people who have just spent ten minutes describing the benefits of a socialist planned, fully nationalised economy, object to money creation as a economic policy because "it will cause inflation." The problem is that it's very simple to understand, and makes sense without needing to check any evidence. Just like the theory that the Sun revolves around the Earth: we can see it with our own eyes.

Keynes disagreed with the theory. In isolation, a massive increase of the money supply, without any other changes occurring as a result, would, in the long run, cause inflation. But as Keynes said, "in the long run, we're all dead." The fact is that spending money causes other changes in the economy, and technology and economic development change the amount and types of goods and services in existence. Extra spending means more customers, more customers means extra production.

The only thing we know for certain about inflation, is that

ZIMBABWE'S HYPERINFLATION

Zimbabwe's hyperinflation took off after 1998 when Zimbabwe intervened in the Second Congo War (until 2003), and at home land was redistributed from white commercial farmers to people without farming experience, often corrupt government officials.

Wheat production collapsed from 300,000 tonnes a year to 50,000. The export tobacco crop fell from US$600mn to US$125mn, thus crippling foreign earnings, and the country was unable to repay its large loans to the IMF that were payable in US dollars.

80% of the population were unemployed. It also had the rife instability and corruption of the Mugabe government. Disease incidence rose and life expectancies fell.

In particular, Zimbabwe only started massively increasing its money supply after all these other factors had already begun the process of hyperinflation.

prices rise when people decide to put them up. Everything else is statistical correlation. In the UK, the broad money supply between 2004 and 2009 increased from £1,190bn to £2,190bn, an increase of 84%. The economy grew from £1,484bn to $1,789bn in that time[30], an increase of 21%. According to the idea that prices are simply the total money divided by the total economic output, prices should have risen by 52%. In fact, prices over the same period increased 14%. You can take any period of years and re-run the calculations. The monetarist theory is demonstrably false in real life timescales.

Inflation is used as a bogeyman to stop socialist policies from being considered. Most socialist economists are highly critical of current **fiscal policy** (taxation and spending decisions) and **monetary policy** (interest rates and money supply decisions). Rather than debate alternatives based on merit, it's much easier to scream, "Ahhg! You'll cause inflation. Look at what happened in Zimbabwe!"

Hyperinflation is when inflation is extremely high. There are different definitions, but typically prices increase by more than 50% each month, making keeping track of what is a fair price for something damn near impossible. It is not accurately explainable using any general, mathematical model of inflation. The psychological mechanisms are what sustains the cycle, not money supply issues, it's essentially a question of people losing trust in a currency. This occurs because of:

- A collapse in real production
- Rampant government corruption
- Loss of a war, or debilitating attritional war
- Regime change or regime collapse
- Loss of control over monetary sovereignty, either because of not having a fiat currency, or having a large debt in a foreign currency.

---

[30] Based on 2009 exchange rates

Historically, hyperinflation only occurs after both significant crashes in real production and massive political instability. There is no law of nature that says Britain couldn't descend into massive civil unrest and experience a collapse of production. But Britain's debt is entirely denominated in Sterling.

Taking control of the money supply to implement expansion of education, modern infrastructure, clean energy generation, better health outcomes, and investment in small businesses and community cooperatives will boost output, not lower it. We should take money creation away from private banks.

Socialism and Business

We are not just here to manage capitalism but to change society and to define its finer values.

- Tony Benn

We've mentioned businesses as essential actors in economic prosperity several times. At first reading, this might sound a bit New Labour or free market. It's not.

All production is social, even for a sole trader. Businesses is the term we use for a team of people organised to do something productive. Just like all successful group dynamics, they have come together for a common purpose. Feel free to use the term enterprise if you you don't like the word business.

In a capitalist free market economy, the purpose of the business is to generate a profit for its share owners. Nine times out of ten, the owners contribute absolutely no work to the production process, and are quite likely to be holding companies of some kind.

But there is no law of nature that says businesses have to be capitalist institutions. The co-operative movement is much larger than most people realise. Innovations in information technology make collaborative ownership and production easier than ever, and most do not require a full-time commitment. As well as your local high street Co-op branch, there are community food co-ops, housing co-ops, and any number of cooperative service industries. Mondragon, in the Basque region of Spain, has a turnover in excess of 12 billion Euros.

Co-ops are something real that can be done today to bring socialism a step closer. They're practical, living proof that another world is possible. If you're haven't already, you should consider joining a local co-op, and maybe also the **Co-operative Party**: you can hold membership of both the Labour and the Co-op Parties at the same time.

If we're successful in winning public support for socialism, we'll also be changing the framework in which businesses operate. Businesses can be publicly owned, but still run as independent organisations by the people who do the work, with input from their customers. The model of centralised, state-owned industries, run remotely by Whitehall committees, does not enjoy a good reputation.

Everything we've seen in other chapters about social psychology, the information flow through distributed networks, and the flow of money, suggests that successful production requires giving those doing the producing the freedom to manage their own affairs and have the freedom to innovate. A large number of heterodox economists, both Post-Keynesian and Marxist, advocate applications of socialism based on autonomous employee-owned and self-managed enterprises.

What we have to change is not operational independence of businesses, but the legal framework and the cultural conception of what a business is. At present, limited companies are (almost always) run with the objective of maximising shareholder value. This could be changed to a legal objective of providing financially sustainable organisations that provide high-quality employment and socially useful goods and services in a socially and environmentally beneficial way. Businesses would be free to collaborate and exchange information without everything being a market transaction reflected on a balance sheet.

For most of us, this would change our lives for the better.

INFRASTRUCTURE

Businesses don't invest in infrastructure for the common good: it's uncompetitive.

There's no reason for one supermarket chain to carry the cost of building a road network if all supermarkets can use it. Or one car manufacturer to set up schools where anyone can learn to read and count (or write poetry or learn history). Maybe if all the supermarkets, and car manufacturers, and building firms, and, well, everyone, invested in physical infrastructure (roads, clean water, power grids, sewerage) and social infrastructure (parks, education, immunisation programmes), then all the firms would benefit. Of course, a few would be tempted to freeload. So why not make the contributions compulsory. And call them tax. And set up agencies that can train staff to take a long term view on these things. And call them state owned assets. Careful, though... we're half way to socialism.

People are generally nervous of change, especially when it comes to earning a living. A method of socialist transformation that begins to show the benefits immediately, and doesn't require upheaval from the familiar routines of daily life, would be the best way to take the wider population with us.

The objective of capitalist businesses is not to produce wealth. It is to produce money. At the height of industrial capitalism, owners used to exploit workers in factories and mines, and sell the goods to make themselves rich.

As it has developed, people motivated to make money have lobbied, bribed and changed the legal and financial system so they can make money without needing to go through the intermediate stage of producing something useful to sell it.

It is not capitalism that produces wealth. Capitalism was never intended to - wealth was only ever a side effect. Wealth, like it always has been, is created by people doing something useful for someone else. In businesses, people cooperate to be far more productive than they are alone.

Socialism, by the way, doesn't automatically include the belief that everyone should get paid the same, regardless of effort. By self-identifying as a socialist, you're signing up the idea that production, distribution and exchange should should be owned or regulated by the community as a whole, and not left to free markets or private, powerful individuals.

We need to trade with each other, and we need the division of labour. In a modern socialist economy, people will still need to eat, and will still want the money to go to the cinema or buy nice wine: there'll be an incentive to work.

The difference is they'll get a lot more freedom of how they do it, and get to keep a much bigger share of the wealth they create, and there'll be a lot more wealth to go round. We don't just want a bigger slice of the cake, we intend to bake a bigger cake.

Profit Motivates People

Economists love to talk about incentives, but the bottom line is that people hate being controlled or manipulated.

- Tyler Cowen

In his 2008 book, **Predictably Irrational**, psychologist and behavioural economist Dan Ariely examined how people make decisions.

The assumption that underpins standard free-market economic theories, and most folk-psychology objections to socialism, is that unless you allow people to become wealthy, no one will innovate.

Neoclassical economics formalises this intuition with the grand title, **Rational Choice Theory**. The idea is that people know precisely what they want, calculate their trade offs - say time worked vs earnings, and then take effective action to bring it about, and that they do it in such a way that economists can draw graphs about it with mathematical precision. How convenient.

It's wrong, and demonstrably so, on the basis of all real-world experimental evidence. Neoclassical economists know it's wrong too, but abandoning it would require abandoning their profession, so they engage in cognitive dissonance reduction, and pretend that it's nearly true.

Many practising economists lean on something called **Bounded Rationality**, which has the same basic framework as rational choice theory, but accepts that in practice, people often have limited access to information, have to make decisions in a time pressured situation, and as such might make sub-optimal choices. It still relies on the basic assumptions that people know what they want and strive to logically achieve it, within the bounds of their capability. It gives them enough wiggle room to explain away the fact that real world observations are at odds with rational choice theory; they can simply say that the evidence happened to show that a sub-optimal decision had been made. Kind of like saying, "God moves in mysterious ways."

Political supporters of free-market policies, along with misanthropes in general, use a folk-psychology version of this to justify policies that undermine any attempt a social cooperation, such as a welfare state, public provision of services and collective democratic oversight of our economy. There are many variations, but the arguments all run something like this: "unless we let the

ALIENATION OF LABOUR

As we saw in the psychology chapters on Self Determination and How People Learn, the most important factors in motivation at work, just as in learning and voluntary activities, are autonomy, competence and meaning.

Giving people the **autonomy** to choose their own way of completing tasks fosters innovation and independence. People are naturally motivated to improve their own performance and gain **competence** and even mastery if they're allowed to. And unless you can see that your work has a point beyond just paying the bills, you'll just go through the motions. **Meaning** doesn't have to be grand: something as simple as delivering all your parcels or emptying the bins has an obvious meaning; being a cog in a clerical machine where you never see the beginning or end of a completed job is soul sapping.

This isn't new. In the 1776 Wealth of Nations, Adam Smith writes about how production line isolation would lead a worker to have "no occasion to exert his understanding, or to exercise his invention... he generally becomes as stupid and ignorant as it is possible for a human creature to become... incapable consequently of forming any just judgement concerning many even of the ordinary duties of private life." His solution was that the government was obliged to remedy this via the subsidised education of children.

In the 1844 Economic and Philosophical Manuscripts, Karl Marx talks about the **Alienation of Labour**, where people are demeaned by their daily work being just a commodity with no meaningful connection to natural human life. His solution was somewhat different to Smith's.

people who work the hardest get the most money, there's no incentive for anyone to work hard, and we all end up poorer."

This is extended by analogy into public services, which results in things like setting up an internal market in the NHS, or privatising the Probation Service.

Aside from the obvious fact that the people who work hardest clearly do not get the greatest share of the wealth (when did you last see a billionaire working an 84-hour week in a Bangladeshi sweat shop?), it is not how people are motivated.

In 2005 Ariely and others were funded by the US Federal Reserve Bank to perform a series of experiments, where they offered people money to perform a variety of tasks. The tasks ranged from the simple, like throwing a ball through a hoop, to solving complex word problems. Different groups were offered differing incentive schemes. Some were asked to do it so the experimenters could benchmark how long things took. Others were told that if they did above average, they'd get a small cash reward. Others were told that if they got in the top range of scores, they'd get a large cash prize.

Standard economic thinking would assume that those groups who were offered more for successful outcomes would achieve the most successful outcomes. Nope. They evidence found exactly the opposite in most cases. When it came to very simple, mechanical tasks, the incentive of more money did result in improved performance. But as soon as a task required even basic cognitive skills (i.e. you had to think about it), an increased financial reward for success led to a decline in performance when compare to groups who were doing the task without financial incentives to succeed.

Ariely and his colleagues wondered if the results were really representative of wider economic behaviour, though, because although offing someone $50 is an incentive, it's not really life-changing to the American students they used as test subjects, and perhaps there were cultural factors at play. So they went to Madurai in rural India, and carried out a similar experiment, this time rewards for success were significant - up to the equivalent of two month's wages. They found the effect was even greater - those not offered extra reward for performance did no worse than those offered a little; and those offered two month's wages if they did well found their performance plummeted on any tasks requiring even basic thinking, planning or judgement.

Paying 19th century ship workers more money to shovel coal faster might be effective; paying 21st century teachers performance-related pay would be a disaster.

The same premise has been tested in other experiments, before and since, for over 50 years, always with the same conclusion. In 2009 Dr Bernd Irlenbush of the LSE reviewed 51 studies, and concluded: "We find that financial incentives can result in a negative impact on overall performance."

Ariely writes about a whole host of other - testable - mechanism about how people make decisions, and that they are largely cultural, or possibly evolutionary, adaptations to maintaining social relationships, not market relationships. Cultural norms and expectations are an order of magnitude more important than incremental, rational-choice style, financial incentives.

In a great RSA Animation[31], Dan Pink summarises the research: "If you don't pay people enough, they won't be motivated. The best use of money as a motivator is to pay people enough to take the issue of money off the table. Pay people enough so they're not thinking about the money, they're thinking about the work." We have to get beyond the ideology of carrots and sticks, and look at the evidence. There is a mismatch between what science knows and what business does.

So next time you hear someone say that competition is necessary to motivate people, ask them if they'd like the fire crew who attend an emergency to compete with each other, or if you'd prefer them to cooperate and work as a team.

[31] Search YouTube: RSA Dan Pink, The surprising truth about what motivates us

Robots

It isn't all over; everything has not been invented; the human adventure is just beginning.

\- Gene Roddenberry

"The economics of the future is somewhat different. The acquisition of wealth is no longer the driving force in our lives. We work to better ourselves and the rest of humanity."

So says Jean Luc Picard in Star Trek, The Next Generation.

In his 1930 essay, Economic Possibilities for our Grandchildren, John Maynard Keynes foreshadowed Picard: mankind's permanent problem is "how to use his freedom from pressing economic cares, how to occupy the leisure, which science and compound interest will have won for him, to live wisely and agreeably and well." He suggested a 15 hour working week would be enough to keep us happy.

In the German Ideology, Karl Marx wrote that under a communist system, a person could "hunt in the morning, fish in the afternoon, rear cattle in the evening, criticise after dinner, just as I have a mind, without ever becoming hunter, fisherman, shepherd or critic."

In 2017 the problem of too much leisure time seems naive. Human innovation has given us plenty of opportunities to busy our minds. The problems are of stress, overwork, economic insecurity, and social isolation.

These problems arise, despite our increased technological productivity, because we have not fixed the problem of how we distribute the extra wealth in a capitalist system. Technology should have given us free time and economic security, but it hasn't. Without redistributive taxation, all the profits simply accumulate to the wealthy. There is widespread concern that increasing automation will lead to technological unemployment and ever greater wealth inequality, rather than across the board increases in lesure time.

In 2013 researchers Carl Benedikt Frey and Michael Osborne published a detailed report that concluded 47% of jobs could be automated in the next two decades. We're on the verge of having driverless cars - the UK has over 200k taxi drivers alone; total driving jobs are in excess of 1m. On the other hand, a driverless van can't deliver your parcel, knock on the door and leave it behind your bin if you're out.

Computer automation isn't new. As writer John Lanchester says, "In the 1960's, mainframe computers churned out bank statements and telephone bills, reducing clerical labour. In the 1970s, memory typewriters replaced repetitive retyping by armies of legal clerks. In the 1980s, PCs with word-wrap were introduced, as were ATMs that replaced bank tellers and barcode scanning that replaced retail workers."

So if productivity has shot up, with so many routine jobs beings replaced by machines like fork-lifts in warehouses and computers in offices, why are we working longer hours, with more people in the workforce, retiring later, then a generation ago?

Where abundance occurs as a result of technological development causing exponential rises in productivity, we have a problem. In capitalism, the whole point of economic activity is to make more money. Making more or better goods and pleasing your customers is not the aim, it's a side effect. So when production becomes so automated that we can afford to give stuff away free, or almost free, how do you make a profit?

The truth is, we're already at this point in certain key industries. At the moment it costs £7.49 a month to get a Netflix subscription, that's £90 a year. How much does it cost Netflix to produce that extra subscription? Nothing. What about the phone calls you make on your phone - does it really cost Vodafone a significant portion of 55p a minute to connect your UK call? No. Capitalism has shifted to finding new ways of extracting cash from society. So today people are employed in telemarketing, or to stand in shopping malls handing out leaflets; we are bombarded by so much digital advertising, that people are (barely) paid to push more junk mail and flyers through your door than ever before.

Coffee is another one. A decade or two ago, you got filter coffee. The staff put it on in advance, and it took a few seconds to pour. Now we have to wait while a minimum-wage barista, probably with a university education, has to grind, tamp, froth and

> **UNIVERSAL BASIC INCOME**
>
> As we saw in the psychology chapters on Self Determination and How People Learn, the most important factors in motivation at work, just as in learning and voluntary activities, are autonomy, competence and meaning.
>
> **Universal Basic Income**, or UBI, is one policy suggestion to deal with increasing automation. The policy is suggested in many forms. The central idea is that everyone from pauper to billionaire gets a fixed monthly income paid by the state, funded by taxation. It's enough to get by, but if you want to have a higher standard of living, you need to earn on top of it. It would free people from having to take exploitative, low paid jobs. If employers want people to work they have to make it worthwhile. It provides a genuine safety net for those who want to study or start businesses.
>
> An alternative suggestion is the **Job Guarantee**. Again, there are various suggestions; the basic concept is that local government would guarantee a living wage job to anyone who wanted one, for as many hours as she cared to work, with full employment rights and benefits, using her skills in an appropriate way.
>
> In either case, though, it would require political will to make it a promising reality, with rates set a level that truly allow economic freedom and security.

steam, mostly in order to justify the cost of the coffee that Starbucks don't pay tax on.

It's one of the most obvious forms of what anthropologist David Graeber calls bullshit jobs, along with advertising executives and corporate lawyers. **Bullshit jobs** aren't all low paid and insecure, though many are. They're jobs that if they weren't done, society would be none the worse. Corporate lawyers, he argues, are just like armies: the only reason you need one is because the other side has one. Millions of jobs involve writing reports or administering forms that no one reads, or would miss if they weren't done. Noticeably, most of these bullshit jobs are in the private sector.

So do capitalist enterprises maintain these bullshit jobs just so people have an income to buy the things other capitalist enterprises have to sell? It seems improbable; there's no causal mechanism that would allow that. It's far more likely to be the fact that industrial productivity is so high that it can support large scale inefficiency in other parts of an organisation, and also because financial capitalism makes such staggering profits independently of any useful activity whatsoever, that it can fund this inefficiency. In short, far from being a either efficient or a conspiracy, neoliberal capitalism is lazy and confused; it barely understands its own system, and is becoming increasing unpredictable and unstable. Many people fall through the gaps, and millions across the world spend their days desperately pretending to do something useful in order to get a small slice of the cake.

It's time for a change. Let's have socialism instead, and organise working lives to do something useful. Then when you've done your work, you can go home, or go out with your mates. If we have meaningful work and decent pay, we'll find a way to enjoy the rest of our time.

History of Capitalism

I am going to fight capitalism even if it kills me. It is wrong that people like you should be comfortable and well fed while all around you people are starving.

- Sylvia Pankhurst

"There is no alternative" was Margaret Thatcher's claim about free market capitalism. It goes hand in hand the persistent myths about human economic interactions over history. Without any recourse to evidence, supporters of free markets assume barter was the basis of early human economic interactions, which proves capitalism is endemic to mankind. However, early humans economies were not based on barter, nor is barter the definition of capitalism.

Throughout pre-industrial history, trade was primarily restricted to long distance trades in physical resources; trade was not the everyday economic activity of individuals. Food, clothing, fuel, tools and shelter were almost entirely produced locally in small communities, with a large degree of reciprocity, where sharing of land, tasks, and produce was regulated by social expectations. In his 2011 book, **Debt: The First 5000 Years**, anthropologist David Graeber calls this "**everyday communism**".

He comprehensively disproves the idea that mankind started with barter, then developed precious metal coins as money, went on to paper money, then systems of debt and credit. The historical evidence shows it was the other way around. Rome had fiat currency from the Emperor Augustus onwards. Humanity's first recorded writings are not religious scripts, but records of who owes what, on clay tablets in Mesopotamia. In 1100, in feudal England, Henry I introduced tally sticks, literally sticks of wood that had the debt obligations carved in them, were then split lengthwise down the grain, so they were virtually unforgeable - the lender kept one, the debtor kept the other. People had to pay their taxes with them; the system remained in use until the 1826. The tally sticks were finally destroyed by burning in 1834, accidentally causing Parliament to burn down.

Capitalism is not the same as trade. It has existed as an economic activity for a long time, if in different formats. The defining characteristic of capitalism is that **the objective is to make money**. If that involves making some useful physical goods as a way of getting the money, then great. If the money can be made by the provision and sale of services, fine. Ditto by lending money at interest, selling insurance, charging people for use of natural monopolies, or dealing in inscrutable financial products like credit default swaps. The point is you start with some money, and then you use it to get more than you started with.

The extent to which this involves the use of violence is secondary from a capitalist point of view. In 1577 Francis Drake, some years before playing bowls and defeating the Spanish, raised money from investors by means of a joint stock syndicate. This was a private venture, funded by a collection of wealthy individuals, and Drake put in £1000 of his own money. Drake & his crew set sail, kidnapped a Portuguese navigator, rounded Cape Horn, and raided towns and captured ships and treasure off South America. It took three years, but he returned home and the loot gathered meant his stock holders got £47 for every £1 invested. Good business.

In December 1600 a Royal Charter established the East India Company, set up with share capital from wealthy Brits. It went on to recruit a private army, 260,000 at its peak, and conquered and ruled India until 1858. The Portuguese, French and Dutch all had East India companies, and ruled most of Indochina. Free market exchanges were not part of the deal for the populations of these lands.

Making money for money's sake is pointless unless there is a substantial market economy - where money can be readily exchanged for things of real use, whether food or housing, or hiring violinists or buying oil paintings. At the height of ancient Rome, these conditions did exist for a small portion of the Empire, and there were money lenders, a simple banking system, and capitalistic enterprises where goods were made just to be sold for money, often by slaves. This represented only a tiny fraction of the Empire's economic output, though. Almost everyone, slave or free, was engaged in subsistence farming, and even taxes were essentially the requisition of goods to be shipped back to central Italy rather than the collection of money. The subsequent decline and fall of Rome and the Pax Romana meant the absence of a market economy until the modern era.

REAL WEALTH

What do the rich do with their extra billions? Do they eat more caviar-stuffed lobsters? No. They invest it to make more. What do they do with the 'more' when they get it? Repeat the cycle. If the investments were all in productive businesses, it wouldn't be so bad. It would be unfair, but at least useful: it would create high quality employment, spur innovation, and generate real wealth as opposed to extra money.

But in real life, they make money by rent-seeking. Their stack of money is increased, but the amount of real wealth - people doing useful, skilled tasks for other people - doesn't change much.

In his 1944 book **The Great Transformation**, Karl Polanyi describes how the modern market economy was brought into creation as an act of political will, in order to enrich and empower a certain strata of society. The rise of industrial technology allowed goods to be produced far in excess of what local populations could use, and they could be traded as commodities. Without a source of labour, though, this industrial system could not work. The enclosure movement completed the picture: land which for centuries had been held in common for the use of people to grow food and graze animals was basically taken off them by act of Parliament, often violently. It had been happening since the 1500s, when raising sheep for wool became more desirable than getting peasants to pay rent in labour or in kind, like cabbages and eggs, and the peasants were forced to migrate, some abroad, some to the towns and cities. If you're a land owner, cabbages and eggs can feed your domestic staff, but wool could be sold to merchants in return for cash to buy silk and brandy.

The process accelerated in the early industrial era. As E.P. Thompson writes in his 1963 **The Making of the English Working Class**, "In agriculture the years between 1760 and 1820 are the years of wholesale enclosure in which, in village after village, common rights are lost." By this point, most of Britain (and also the Netherlands) was a market economy, where few people grew their own food, and food was acquired by monetary exchange.

Wage labour is not an essential feature of capitalism, at least in principle. Paid labour is fertile ground for capitalism, but not its only source of profit. There's no incompatibility between slavery and capitalism, as shown by the American (and indeed worldwide) slave-worked plantations of the 1500's to 1800's.

The idea that capitalism is about industrial production and the expropriation of surplus value, i.e. not paying workers the full value of their work, is incomplete. Industrial capitalism is just one form of capitalism, and because of the attention it received from Marx, who was in part writing (in many works) to refute economists in the tradition of Adam Smith, people have extrapolated it to represent all of capitalist activity. It never was; even in the peak of the factory era, more people worked outside of manufacturing than inside it: domestic servants, shop workers, sailors, dock workers, clerks, prostitutes, market stall holders, not to mention farm workers. They were not producing commodities.

Nor are all capitalist profits the direct appropriation of surplus value. Moneylenders make money off interest, stockbrokers make money of rising asset prices, and landlords and other rent seekers make money by charging for existing assets. A major contemporary source of rent seeking is PFI buildings - a rigged system was created in the Major years, and massively expanded by New Labour. By getting wealthy financiers to stump up some of the cash to build a new school, hospital or government office, deals were struck where the public was contracted to pay inflated "service charges" for decades. The £12bn used to fund hospitals will cost us £79bn over 30 years.

Individual capitalists don't need the entire system to balance out - the idea that the workers can't afford to buy the goods they make is not a concern for the individual firm. Indeed, many go bust: capitalism is an inherently messy, wasteful system: the market is essentially trial and error, which is why so few capitalists accept free markets, whenever they have the power, they rig them. The entire sovereign debt crisis and bank bail out is exactly because the working people can't earn enough to pay for the profits of the wealthy, so we just create ever more money in the form of debt, which finds its way into the hands of the already rich.

Thomas Piketty describes the process of ever increasing wealth inequality in **Capital in the Twenty-First Century**, saying the concentration of wealth in fewer and fewer hands is inevitable, unless rises in productivity outstrip the rate of return on capital. In other words, the system has to grow faster than the profits that are made, or it fails.

The lesson of history is that people are quite capable of coming together to produce useful goods and services without needing to have a profit motive. We're used to money, we've used it for milllennia, it's easy to use, and we'll continue to use money for exchange in a complex, interconnected economy. But the NHS, and schools the world over, and indeed all modern militaries, work just fine without needing to turn a profit. As soon as we introduce a profit motive, human ingenuity is tempted away from the innovative provision of useful things, towards ways of making a quick buck, whatever the cost to others.

Socialism is not just about fairness, but also about long-term economic sustainability.

Postcapitalism, Socialism and Neofeudalism

The lightbulb changed the world; Facebook is just a way of letting people click 'like' on photos of cats that resemble Colonel Gaddafi.

- John Lanchester

It has become easier to imagine the end of the world than the end of capitalism. So said cultural theorist Fredric Jameson.

Since the Thatcher era and the fall of the Berlin Wall, the British socialist movement, like most of the rest of the world, has focused on opposing things, engaging in defensive battles to protect gains of the past against neoliberal states and corporations. Where progress has been made is in the areas of gender equality and gay rights, and to some extent, a reduction of racism.

In the 17th and 18th centuries we saw the rise of mercantile and slave capitalism; in the 19th and 20th centuries we saw the rise of industrial capitalism. We now have the information capital of the 21st century. The old activities still exist - we still transport spices around the globe, and we still smelt iron; but they're no longer the profit centres they once were. Aside from the massively unbalancing financial sector, profitability for capitalism comes from information.

Consider Uber. Getting accurate statistics is difficult, partly because they keep changing, and partly because of deliberate obfuscation. They have a global turnover of maybe $6bn, and keep ~20% of what their customers pay, with the rest going to the drivers. This sucks money out of local economies, reducing local demand, and puts it in the tax havens of the rich even quicker than previously.

But what, actually, do companies like Uber do for their money? It looks like they produced a smartphone app, and a software system that matches that with drivers, so you can hail a cab. Mostly, though, their operating costs are legal and lobbying: trying to extend and protect their monopoly on the smartphone taxi business. If you think about it, the only thing stopping local authorities doing the same thing is intellectual property law.

Airbnb operates on a similar model. Only slightly different are TripAdvisor, Facebook, Amazon and Google. They're all versions of what are sometimes called **Platform Capitalism**. **Network orchestrators** have been a capitalist business model since the railways or post services. But in the digital age, they need no infrastructure of their own, and have zero marginal costs. Delivering more letters meant more postmen and women; showing more Facebook ads needs - what, exactly? Nothing Facebook pays for.

Would we have to ban Google, Facebook or Uber? No. We could simply put a 90% turnover tax on digital network orchestrators that turn over more than £1bn. They'd still trade; it costs them nothing to extend their operations in one more country, and 10% is better than 0%. If they spit out the dummy, someone else would soon occupy that commercial space. Unlike profit taxes, you can't use clever accountancy to offshore your turnover.

The marginal cost of production of anything you can copy and paste is close to zero. Sure, the first one needs a lot of skilled labour, possibly a huge team. But the second, third, and ten millionth are basically free. So the only thing stopping us from making information products free is political protection of private property. But in most of these cases, the information that gives them their value came from us: if only ten people downloaded Uber, it would be worthless.

Much more is information than we realise. The value of almost all advanced manufactured goods is in their information content. Basic commodities like wheat, steel, oil and timber have

TALK SOCIALISM

In order to build a better world, we must first imagine it.

This is what Talk Socialism, and this book, is all about. We don't want to write a manifesto and campaign on it. We want to encourage and enable people to come together in a networked way, to share skills and insights, and to start to build an alternative within the current system.

That involves learning what's possible, how people change their behaviour, how best to communicate ideas.

As Paul Mason says, "We need a project based on reason, evidence and testable designs, that cuts with the grain of history and is sustainable by the planet. And we need to get on with it."

to be harvested and processed. Most of the sale value, though, is in the R&D of complex products, everything from pharmaceuticals to jet engines. In most cases, the costs of research are borne substantially by the public sector and higher education institutions.

In his 2015 book, **PostCapitalism: A Guide to our Future**, Paul Mason says, "Today, the thing that is corroding capitalism, barely rationalised by mainstream economics, is information. Most laws concerning information define the right of corporations to hoard it and the right of states to access it, irrespective of the human rights of citizens." This has exacerbated the tendency for capitalist profits to move away from productive manufacturing or efficient service provision, and towards either platform capitalism - like Uber and Google, or financial capitalism.

The thing is, these high profit companies don't employ many people. They barely need to employ any at all - the actual labour elements could be subcontracted. "The main contradiction today is between the possibility of free, abundant goods and information; and a system of monopolies, banks and governments trying to keep things private, scarce and commercial. Everything comes down to the struggle between the network and the hierarchy: between old forms of society moulded around capitalism and new forms of society that prefigure what comes next."

It's worth noting that Mason isn't prophesying an imminent overthrow or final crisis of capitalism. The core of his thesis is that what needs to be done to change society is different from the industrial battles of the 19th and 20th century. "If I am right, the logical focus for supporters of postcapitalism is to build alternatives within the system; to use governmental power in a radical and disruptive way; and to direct all actions towards the transition – not the defence of random elements of the old system. We have to learn what's urgent, and what's important, and that sometimes they do not coincide."

"Bourgeois society stands at the crossroads, either transition to Socialism or regression into Barbarism," wrote Rosa

Luxemburg in 1916[32]. She was very nearly right - the boom of the 1920s was short lived, the crash of 1929 led to widespread unemployment throughout the world, the rise of Fascism across Europe simultaneous with murderous Stalinism in Russia. The allied victory in WWII was not inevitable.

If we don't succeed, the possible future could be **neofeudalism**, where the widening of the wealth gap sees the poor and marginalised excluded from the state's provision of security. Not just our access to justice and expensive lawyers, but actually different legal rights depending upon your ability to pay or where you can afford to live.

The use of private police forces is widespread in the US and South Africa, with gated communities. It's not hard to imagine legal powers being extended to these companies, and then we're only a small step away from private courts. The UK already has private prisons and a 70% privatised probation service.

We're seeing debt bondage forced onto young people simply for wanting a higher education; a necessary economic risk if you want a well paid career. Will the future be, that when you turn 18, you get a bill for your primary education, that you pay off for the next forty years? In the mean time, CompuGlobalHyperMegaNet gets the right to monitor all your communications, your whereabouts, medical records and conversations, in order to sell the data to the highest bidder?

When we add in the very real ecological crisis that individual capitalist enterprises have no motivation to address, and the megabucks made from the military-industrial complex, the dangers of a dystopian future are not hypothetical.

Mason argues that just as the modern economy is distributed and digital, so is the solution. "By creating millions of networked people, financially exploited but with the whole of human intelligence one thumb-swipe away, info-capitalism has created a new agent of change in history: the educated and

[32] She was quoting Freiderich Engels's early use of the phrase

connected human being.... The design of the postcapitalist world, as with software, can be modular. Different people can work on it in different places, at different speeds, with relative autonomy from each other. It is the elites – cut off in their dark-limo world – whose project looks as forlorn as that of the millennial sects of the 19th century. The democracy of riot squads, corrupt politicians, magnate-controlled newspapers and the surveillance state looks as phoney and fragile as East Germany did 30 years ago."

Participatory Politics

Top-down chains of command are not particularly efficient: they tend to promote stupidity among those on top and resentful foot-dragging among those on the bottom. The greater the need to improvise, the more democratic the cooperation tends to become.

- David Graeber

As long as there have been complex human societies, people have liked stories about heroes.

It's an expression of many things: wish fulfilment, helplessness, tribal identity, and simple narrative appeal. In our modern society, with an overwhelming deluge of soap operas, period dramas, action films, police procedurals, and so on, we've been almost brainwashed to think that we're consumers of stories.

Many moral and sincere socialists still subconsciously accept the model that our role is to get our guy or girl elected, and he or she will deliver socialism on our behalf.

Think again. It's a logical impossibility.

The only way to achieve socialism is with a broad, deep and capable layer of leaders at every level. Socialism is social: it's about people. Local, grassroots leaders are needed at every level. Not every one of those leaders needs to be a philosophical theorist or an economics guru. But every area of every town and city needs someone that people recognise as a trustworthy representative, someone who can articulate the basic points of inclusive, democratic socialism; someone who can help newcomers take those early steps to contributing to a better way of running our society.

Participatory politics is about participation on multiple levels. Participation is not just about showing up to meetings. It's about being active when you turn up, rather than passive. Custom and practice, and our school-based education system, have fostered two models in most political activities, whether rallies, organising meetings, education sessions, or even street & community activities.

The first is the bureaucratic committee model. It's like any meeting in most workplaces. The better ones are well chaired and have an agenda. But they're all dull, and even motivated activists attend them from a sense of duty rather than enjoyment. By and large they drain the enthusiasm of newcomers faster than water on the desert sands. The primary cause is that people have meetings to talk about what to do, rather than having meetings to actually do. They do this because it's always been done like that, or because it's easier to follow a rule book or a habit than it is to be imaginative.

The second is the performer - audience model. When we go to a play or a music gig to see someone else perform, we expect to sit and evaluate, not to create. Most political education meetings are like this, most rallies, and many campaigning activities. One person, or a panel, has the socially implied role of experts, and everyone else defaults into audience mode. The problem is that it wastes 95% the brain power and imagination in the room.

Until we break this mould, and establish a culture and expectation that we all expect to be doing something constructive in political meetings, we'll never develop the thousands of grassroots leaders we need.

There is an alternative. We could practice what we preach, and decide that the "strength of our common endeavour..." applies to how we build for socialism. We could decide that politics can be fun, and about people - not just meeting our political goals for people (better housing, fairer wealth distribution...), but about building camaraderie and tapping into the humour and creativity of each other along the way. You never know - people might surprise you.

The Authentic Self

If we're going to be damned, let's be damned for what we really are

- Jean-Luc Picard

It's be much easier to be yourself than it is to be somebody else. You've had more practice. Yet when we join groups or find ourselves in different social contexts we tend to adopt personas, usually to meet the expectations of the group, and perhaps to win acceptance and approval.

Politics gets very tribal. Too often, well motivated political activists who would never engage in racist or sexist labelling engage in the factional stereotyping of political opponents. Often other trends in the Labour movement come in for harsher criticism than the Tory party do. It's a barrier to winning more people to our ideas.

Philosopher Jean Paul Sartre developed the concept of mauvaise foi, or **Bad Faith**. We've all done it at some point or another, where we act in accordance with the role we have, rather than from our own, considered, authentic beliefs. Most of us have known a boss who was a perfectly reasonable person outside work, but felt compelled to act the role of a boss at work. Most parents have been tempted to exhort the platitudes they heard as kids, like "because I said so" or "you'll have somebody's eye out with that" and then wondered why on Earth they said something so inane.

Simone de Beauvoir describes the **Serious Man**, one who denies his own freedom and subjugate it to higher values. He (or she) is so wrapped up in his cause he is in Bad Faith because he forgets he has a choice about how to behave at every juncture. The Serious Man of politics feels he has to rebut every comment; he sees everything through the spectrum of his cause. He forgets that people could be making causal remarks, or may change their minds. He forgets to see others as authentic people, and sees them as their labels.

If you're authentic with other people, they're more likely to be authentic with you. Always be a first-rate version of yourself, instead of a second-rate version of somebody else.

CHARISMA AND AUTHENTICITY

Despite what spin doctors think, the most reliable way to persuade someone is not to tell them what they want to hear, but to tell them what you sincerely believe.

When you start altering your behaviour or your message to fit the expectations of other people, you've become needy. And it shows. If you're authentic (and also polite and witty) you'll get respect and be taken more seriously.

It's worth saying, directly, "I don't mind if you think differently from me, but what I'm telling you is the truth as I see it."

Sustainable Activism

You can't sustain a high level of intense activity with thousands of people forever. It has to be for a specific objective.

- Jeremy Corbyn

Socialist activism is a bit like housework. Once you start doing it, you realise there's more to do than you ever imagined. In fact, you could spend your life doing it and never be finished.

There are tens of thousands of activists in the UK, many of whom might not even self-identify as socialists, but who participate in voluntary organisations to make a better world, campaigning on issues like climate change, unionisation of workplaces, or the arms trade; participating in local democracy through the Labour or Green Party; or engaged in community activism, like foodbanks or community co-ops.

Over the past few years, hundreds of thousands more have joined in with political activity, particularly since Jeremy Corbyn made it on to the ballot paper for the Labour leadership in 2015. It turns out that the ideas of socialism were alive and well, and people just needed a focal point.

Huge numbers of these people don't have the time to commit to a high level of activism. Between demos, attending Labour Party meetings, campaigning meetings, street stalls, door knocking, community activism.... it's a recipe for burnout. In particular, those who already have established lives, perhaps a little older, with kids, full time jobs, and rooted with other social commitments can feel that activism is just not possible for them. An activist is someone who sees herself as an actor, not as part of the audience. It's understandable that busy people see themselves as part of the audience, cheering on the likes of Corbyn and his activist supporters, but don't see themselves as actors on the stage of history.

If we're going to build enough people power to make the transition to socialism a reality we have to answer this question:

How can someone with two free evenings a month be a socialist activist?

Whether you're an activist organiser looking to make it easier for people to participate, or one of those with barely enough time to watch the news never mind turn up to committee meetings, here are a few ideas.

1. **Do something you enjoy**. When we see an injustice or a high-profile cause, like an election campaign, the initial surge of emotion is enough to get us through the humdrum that goes with the terrain. Months later, when the cold rainy nights set in, unless we're looking forward to the activity for its own sake, we'll stop.

2. **Do something you're good at**, or want to get better at. Curiosity and the drive for mastery runs deep in human psychology. There are few things that are more satisfying than knowing you've done a good job, or seeing yourself develop a new skill.

3. **Do something that puts you in touch** with other people, and connects you new networks. If there are a million people who all think the same but don't know anyone else who thinks so too, then nothing happens. The power of a network grows as it has more connections, the same is true for social networks.

It could be that you spend one evening a month at a socialist reading group. This is more valuable to activism than might be first apparent. Democratic socialism can't be imposed from above, it needs large numbers of people to know what the ideas mean, and how to engage in an informed debate on matters of economics and political philosophy.

The network effect of having a mass, articulate socialist movement, where in every community there is someone who could easily refute the myths of neoliberal capitalism, would transform the political landscape. Long term, it's by changing the terms of political discourse that societies change.

A socialist film club would have similar benefits, and at one community organising workshop we ran recently, someone suggested a Socialist Sunday School[33] for families.

It could be that you go along to your local Labour branch or CLP meeting just once a year, but say hello to people and ask them to keep in touch about other events that suit your calender better. When you do go along, don't sit passively waiting for

[33] A Socialist Sundae School would be even more popular.

DONE IS BETTER THAN PERFACT

We use this phrase a lot. As volunteers in political activity, we have to accept that our time is limited. Far better to accomplish something modest today than to still be thinking about starting something ambitious tomorrow. You can build on your accomplishments. It's hard to build on your ambitions.

someone to welcome you. It would be great if organisers always made the effort to spend time with new members, but they're probably distracted by all the other tasks they have to do, and they are almost certainly volunteers too. So introduce yourself, say you're busy most evenings and weekends, but you'll help when you can.

The face to face contact matters. Social media has indeed changed the landscape, but it hasn't changed human psychology much. It's only the close contact that builds the trust and camaraderie that's needed.

Before we set up Talk Socialism, we sat around and deliberated about what we should do. Jeremy Corbyn had just won the 2015 Labour leadership election, and hundreds of thousands of new people had joined or come back to socialist politics, and we wanted to make a difference in some way. We're all volunteers with busy lives, families and full time jobs - we don't get paid for running Talk Socialism, we have no staff. We decided that we needed to do something sustainable, that we'd continue to enjoy, and that would not become a chore.

So we decided on political education and training for that reason - we love the ideas, the workshops, hearing different perspectives, learning things from the people we meet. For you, it might be something else. Whatever it is, make sure it's about the people as much as it's about the cause. That way, you'll meet brilliant people, and that's the most sustainable thing of all.

Leadership Styles

You don't need to hold a position to be a leader.

- Henry Ford

Leadership is the biggest seller for corporate training courses; loads of people want to better at it, and yet the range of advice and exercises on the subject could fill libraries. The main reason there's so much differing advice is because most of it is ineffective. Not because it's bad advice, but because it often won't work in the context that people try to apply it.

In the corporate world, leadership is very rarely welcomed. Mostly, people further up the chain would prefer you to manage people and projects rather than lead them. Leadership is not the same thing as management. When it comes to budgets and deadlines, management is probably more useful than leadership in the short term.

We're not interested here in what makes a good general or CEO or Prime Minister. We're talking about what leadership is in the context of grassroots political activity. Our old friend Kurt Lewin (from the psychology section) was one of the first to define leadership styles, back in 1939. There are many models, but this is a good starting place.

Authoritarian leaders impose their judgements on the group, often without any consultation, and tend to limit opportunities for discussion. They see themselves as judges and arbiters. They tend to demand rules are followed, often on a arbitrary basis. They like to assign tasks, and rarely seek consensus. In grassroots participatory politics, these kinds of leaders have very few followers, and those they do have are very dogmatic, with their affinity based on a strong in-group identity.

There are two main reasons why people are authoritarian. One is cultural: they believe that's what a leader is supposed to be like, and confuse leadership with dictatorship. They often genuinely believe a strong, decisive leader is what's needed. The second main reason is the result of a lack of confidence. People hide behind their badge because on some level they feel they can't meet the expectations of others, and use the office to justify their decisions. These two reasons are not mutually exclusive.

Authoritarian leadership sometimes arises from a lack of personal leadership ability. Leaders who lack experience or self-awareness often assume that other people agree with them, or will accept their judgements, and are surprised when others don't. They attribute this to divisiveness, use autocratic methods, and feel justified in doing so.

If you know someone who is an autocratic leader, it might be worth developing a channel of communication where you can raise the question in a non-confrontational way. Asking a causal question can help: "Why do you think Bob keeps objecting to your decisions, do you think? "

In some cases, though, autocratic leaders lack even enough self-awareness for this.

Democratic leaders gain their authority by being seen to empower the collective will of the group. Accountability is achieved through dialogue rather than just formal mechanisms like votes: effective facilitation teases out the creative talents of the group, builds a consensus, and gains the consent of all concerned. It involves communicating with people over extended time periods, not just through meetings, and build up networks of communication and trust. It requires seeking out people with specialist knowledge and making sure their experience is shared with the group as part of the decision making process. Gaining trust also requires turning up and doing the work.

Effective facilitation means getting to the point: letting people do a Grandpa Simpson and ramble on for ages is not democratic leadership, it's an absence of leadership.

DO WE GET THE LEADERS WE DESERVE?

In the Knowledge Illusion, Steve Sloan and Philip Fernbach talk about the role of shared knowledge in the context of political leadership: "Strong leaders make use of the community of knowledge by surrounding themselves with people who have a deep understanding of specific issues. A leader who spends significant time collecting information and talking to others before making a decision can be seen as indecisive, weak, and lacking vision. A mature electorate is one that makes the effort to appreciate a leader who recognises that the world is complex and hard to understand."

In groups that don't need innovation or growth, there's little need for democratic leadership. Either the group has few difficult or creative decisions to make, or else everyone knows what they're doing and can get on with it. If a group is trying to grow, develop new people, and, in short, win campaigns for socialist causes, democratic leadership is needed. Importantly, democratic leadership doesn't all have to reside in one person, you can job share.

Lassaiz-faire leadership is a very hands off approach. In the context of participatory politics, it's what happens when someone is in a leadership position and does very little with it, leaving the group to take all initiatives and make all decisions. The Lassaiz-faire leader oversees the formal decision making process, but basically lets everyone take their turn, then puts it to a vote.

For some established groups operating in a steady state, it may be what's required - such as a long running food co-op or community litter picking group. If a group needs dynamism, though, it's a poor approach - new people tend to defer to those already in positions, and the lack of leadership causes them to drift away fairly quickly.

Grassroots leadership is not about being in charge, and it's not about office holding. It's about being someone other people come and ask when they want help, advice, or a second opinion. It's about stepping in when there's doubt or indecision and suggesting a positive course of action that leads somewhere. It's about setting the tone and culture of the group, and facilitating clear communication. It's about letting people make their own minds up, making sure they're aware of what others think too. It's about remembering what it was like when you first came along, didn't know anyone, and were naive and cocksure and terrified all at the same time. It requires genuine affection for the people you're leading, and remembering they're human and have faults, and a willingness to admit that so do you. It's not significantly different from being a good, enlightened parent[34].

[34] Fewer nappies, though.

The Leadership Gap

You choose your leaders and place your trust,

As their lies wash you down and their promises rust.

- The Jam

It's worth clarifying some of the language around leadership.

Positional leadership is where you have authority because of the office you hold. In political activity, that's usually because you've been elected to a position. That election may have been by default, if no one stood against you, or if you set up the group. It could have been a contested election, and possibly many of those who voted against you disagree with you on questions significant to the office. Positional leadership can give people confidence from the implied authority - often people are reluctant to take actions because of the way they see themselves - they don't consider themselves empowered. So giving someone an office can help empower them.

In most cases, though, holding an office gives you no **personal leadership**. In almost all cases beyond routine administration, people will only listen to you, seek and follow your advice on the basis of your personal qualities and conduct. Effective grassroots leadership requires developing strong personal leadership skills. The ability to listen to others, find common ground and sift the genuine disagreements from the superficial. It involves having a vision for how to achieve the group's goals, and being able to communicate that vision on the level of both the big picture and the immediate tasks.

Even in democratic, participatory politics, it is self-evident that we are not all equal in knowledge, experience and ability. People have different skill sets, some know the lie of the land, and have more connections and contacts than others. It's natural for people to defer to the opinion of others on a case by case basis. In fact, helping each other and sharing our skills is the basis of socialism.

A problem occurs when people leave tasks to leaders, especially positional leaders. It's analogous to the wealth gap. The more wealth inequality a society has, the more investment decisions are taken by a smaller number of people, and the less that society's talents are used.

WHY DON'T YOU DO X?

Almost without exception, at every meeting we attend, someone will speak up from the room and ask the organisers, "why don't you organise a meeting on..." or "produce a newsletter on..." or some other suggestion. The ideas are often very good, but the implication isn't.

In our corporate consumer society, many people who come to socialist events still behave as consumers, just of political activity. Our collective challenge is to get people to see themselves differently - to see themselves not as the audience, but as political actors.

Whenever someone asks us "Why don't you do X?" we reply, sincerely, "Good idea, thanks for volunteering. Would you like us to help you with that?"

Political leadership follows the same pattern. In organisations where the mass of the membership are passive, and the initiatives come from a top strata, the less effective that organisation is for its size.

It's not just an issue about democracy. It's a direct consequence of people not being in the loop. If you delegate not only decision making, but deliberations about the decision making to small elite, even if democratically elected, everyone else drifts off and does other things. We see it in voting behaviour, where the levels of political ignorance are rife amongst huge numbers of otherwise intelligent, capable citizens. We're not talking about marginalised people, we're making the simple case that even astute people become ignorant about a subject unless they're actively involved in it.

In the case of political activity, the more you delegate decisions to hierarchical bodies, the more an organisation will atrophy.

The Labour movement grew up as a reaction to the injustices of the corporate world. Ironically, many of the traditional organisational models of the Labour movement follow the same structure. An effective socialist movement capable of changing societies will have to be pluralist, diverse and distributed, with lots of people taking their own initiatives with their colleagues. It will have to intentionally have a wide variety of ways for people to participate, and we have to abandon the obsession with being "on message". We can agree a set of core policies, and be honest that there's an open debate around others.

There's no use in electing a great, socialist leader of the Labour Party unless we step up and lead with him[35].

---

[35] Or her - who knows who'll follow Jezza?

What Makes a Good Session

If people never did silly things nothing intelligent would ever get done.

- Ludwig Wittgenstein

An old hand talks to a new member of the Labour Party.

"Do you want to come to our meeting?"

"Okay, what will happen?"

"The chair will run through the agenda, then we'll take apologies, then we'll look at the minutes of the previous meeting..."

Oh, blimey, that sounds less interesting than being at work. "What difference will it make if I'm there?"

"Hmm, I hadn't really thought of that. I guess it'll make us feel like things are going well."

"Will I get to discuss Labour Party policy?"

"Ah, no. We don't do that."

"Will I get a chance to persuade my MP which way to vote on an issue that matters to me?"

"Erm...."

"So, I'll be meat in the room, then."

"No, you need to accept that it's a case of delayed gratification. You turn up every month, deliver some leaflets, knock a few doors at election time for your local councillor, then your MP..."

"The one who I don't get to talk to?"

"...that's not exactly fair, some of them do make the effort, although not all of them, it's true. Anyway, then, every generation or so, when a sitting MP retires, you get to vote for the replacement."

"But don't I get to vote for the replacement even if I don't turn up for all the minutes and matters arising and leafleting and stuff?"

A pause. *"Please come along."*

"I get delayed gratification, I do. I'm intelligent, and engaged, I read things, I understand why politics matters. But I'm just not motivated enough to sit through years of being an extra in someone else's drama unless it's interesting. Unless it engages my intellect or my emotions."

A longer pause.

"We have a raffle."

Rachel hates raffles with a passion. They embody everything that represents inertia in politics. It's hard to think of an activity that's further away from the reason people become motivated to participate in socialist politics. Right down to the outcome being decided by fate.

In Talk Socialism we've experimented with what makes a good session - training workshop, reading group, planning & decision making meetings - so we're going to try and convey our findings in a few hundred words.

A good session needs energy, interactive participation, positive action, and meaningful goals. Unfortunately that gives the acronym EIPPAMG, so we changed it to:

Zing

Interaction

Positive

Significant

When you get the elements right, the whole thing ZIPS together! Now we sound like real management consultants. :-)

Zing - energy - humour - spirit - bravado - a touch of derring do. This is self-evident - if you're leading a session, and you have all the wit and charm of a medical questionnaire, people will get bored. If you want people to give up their time to come to your sessions, have the courtesy to be engaging. It sounds obvious, but many people don't do it, either from habit, or because they're nervous being in the spotlight.

You don't have to be witty, but if you are, that's handy. Start with a big, friendly hello. Set the tone. Say why you're there - why it matters to you, why you enjoy it. If someone says something you like, acknowledge it and agree with them. If you're a fundamentally unlikeable person, you won't be able to do this. Everyone else can - be yourself. And don't do it alone. We always design our sessions so that at least two people are facilitating them.

It's not a one way street, though. Always give the group a chance to contribute to the zing. It might be as simple as asking them, "Who's got a positive experience they want to share?" You'll hear some great stories from people, and some great ideas. If you're enjoying the session, it'll show, and others probably will too.

Interaction is the part that most political sessions get wrong. You might have a dozen, twenty, fifty people at a meeting, and they all take it turn to speak, and have to make all their points in one go, then someone else does the same. That's not interaction; it is taking it in turns to make speeches, a totally unnatural form of dialogue that cuts across the grain of normal human interactions rather than cutting with it.

People communicate best in small groups. In sessions, we try to avoid getting people in pairs, as occasionally two people have very different communication styles and then sit in awkward silence. So we get groups of three to four, and have short periods of discussion, then switch the groups around, so ideas get developed. This massively increases the bandwidth of the discussion, and engages 100% of the people there in a real dialogue, with a real, flowing conversation.

We don't then get the groups to feed back. This is just another form of unnatural communication, where you're

BANDWIDTH

Imagine you've got fifty people in a room, and you record the session. In a standard panel or speaker Q&A, where people speak one at a time after being called by the chair, after one hour you'd have about 50 minutes of speech. Some of it might be very good, but most of it could be gained watching a video or podcast.

Imagine instead you get those fifty people to spend their time talking to each other. The network effect is huge. In one hour you'd likely have 500 to 1000 minutes of speech, and everyone would have developed their thoughts through a process of dialogue.

Let's take the brakes off, and make our movement truly collaborative.

kind of obliging the designated feedback giver to list everything that was said, out of context, while everyone else sits around waiting for their turn to talk. Instead we ask for something more spontaneous: did anyone hear anything that made them think "Wow! Great idea?"

In workshops, we always have games that are linked to the skills we're practising. We use large group role-play, small group role-play, quizzes, exercises where people have to summarise a point in ten seconds, communication exercises, policy sharing, recording videos on smart phones, and a host of other things. Get in touch if you want to collaborate on developing a specific training session.

Positive actions are essential, and as facilitators you have to actively encourage this. The tendency in groups is to start by enumerating all the things they don't like. It can feel good to get it off your chest, but it's not much fun for those listening. Be explicit that we're looking for solutions, not more problems. If it's about a specific campaign or policy area, then there is likely much to complain about - the actions of the Tory government, for instance. But a session entirely about how bad the Tories are is actually pretty demotivational. Misery loves company[36].

Instead, spend your time focusing on what you can do about it, or how you can develop counter arguments to win the public debate. Then practice those arguments, there and then. Have people leave the meeting with a positive focus of what they can do, and they might just do it.

Significant, meaningful goals are the reason you're there in the first place. Socialism is about society-wide change on a generational timescale. It requires a lot of faith in our collective ability to sustain activism for years on the basis of ideas alone.

As we covered in the chapters on learning and work, it is meaning that drives our progress. Design sessions to have clear, useful, well defined outcomes. It could be to decide on the next community campaign, in which case outline a sketch plan, get

[36] And quite often insists upon it.

people to volunteer for roles, and decide the next step. It could be a political education session to get an understanding of the last financial crash. In which case, include time for people to practice articulating what they've learned, so they go away feeling they can explain it, and not just a vague feeling of being more knowledgeable.

If you've done a good session, after people come away from it, they will see themselves slightly differently from how they did before. They might be more motivated, more knowledgeable, more skilled, or feel part of a stronger collective. They'll see themselves as capable of taking action that can make a difference.

Clicktivism, Activism, or Talk Socialism

It is the long history of humankind (and animal kind, too) those who learned to collaborate and improvise most effectively have prevailed.

- Charles Darwin

We've already written about the role of the individual in networks, and how groups are stronger with more autonomous, networked individual participants.

This has manifested in something of a debate about clicktivism vs activism. In the UK, the pressure group 38 Degrees paved the way by making it easy to join a campaign by signing an online petition. They weren't the first to engage people online or with petitions, Amnesty International, Greenpeace, and War on Want, to name three, have been fighting their corners with some success for decades. But 38 degrees did something new: they had no stated goals or policy aims of their own. They were the Facebook of politics; they provided the platform, the users created the content. And good luck to them, they've had an effect.

After the Corbyn surge, there was much talk about fair-weather supporters; a small number of Labour MPs were really very scathing about keyboard warriors people who only do things on social media but never turned up to meetings. The real work was to be done on doorsteps. It wasn't just the establishment of the Labour Party, either; ironically some Marxist-Leninist groups weren't happy with Momentum's path of making decisions by online ballots.

It's a false dichotomy, as many are starting to see. Whether it's how we shop, or how we talk to our friends and families, very few of us don't have a foot in both camps. We chat on Facebook or email, and we also go out face-to-face for a beer. We do it because we can, and for some things one method is better than the other.

Political activism is affected by this shift, and it has an impact on how we should see the boundaries of groups and organisations. The Labour Party, for example, still has a structure that dates from the Edwardian era. By having a rigid pyramidal structure based on local authority ward boundaries, it has shackled itself to geographical boundaries that bear little relation to the actual communities and social networks that exist. The chances of you and your best mates all living in the same ward area are slim, so you can't go along to meetings together. It needs to change, and in most cases, people unofficially self-organise on a different basis anyway.

People no longer see a need to be in just one organisation either, especially since it's easier to communicate without turning up. Just as they might thumb swipe to get news from different sources, they can participate in different ways, going to a meeting of one group, a demo organised by another, and sharing the posts

JUNGLE SCHOOL BOARD

When the animals decided to establish schools they selected a school board consisting of Mr. Elephant, Mr. Kangaroo and Mr. Monkey, and these fellows held a meeting to agree upon their plans.

"What shall the animals' children be taught in the animal school? That is the question," declared Mr. Monkey.

"Yes, that is the question," exclaimed Mr. Kangaroo and Mr. Elephant together.

"They should be taught to climb trees," said the monkey, positively. "All my relatives will serve as teachers."

"No, indeed!" shouted the other two, in chorus. "That would never do."

"They should he taught to jump," cried the kangaroo, with emphasis. "All of my relatives will be glad to teach them."

"No, indeed!" yelled the other two, in unison. "That would never do."

"They should be taught to look wise," said the elephant. "And all of my relatives will act as teachers."

"No, indeed!" howled the other two together. "That will never do."

"Well, what will do?" they asked, as they looked at each other in perplexity.

"Teach them to climb," said Mr. Monkey.

"Teach them to jump," said Mr. Kangaroo.

"Teach them to look wise," said Mr. Elephant.

And so it was that none of them would yield, and when they saw there was no chance to agree, they all became angry and decided not to have any animal schools at all.

From The Jungle School Board, 1903

from a third.

Despite this reality, many political organisers still suffer from what we call **Party Envy**, like socialites who are disappointed if you go to someone else's party and not theirs. The reasons are often the same, they're tying up their ego with the success of their structures[37]. What matters is whether there's a longer term benefit.

As far as possible, we try to collaborate with other groups. Just as networks of autonomous individuals build stronger, more creative, more productive groups, networks of autonomous groups build stronger, more creative, more productive movements. The main initial barrier is party envy; people get protective over brand identities in a way that would embarrass most corporate marketing directors. Beyond that, just like with individuals in groups, it's a case of finding what goals there are that we can both achieve better together, and then start working on them. Leave the other goals out of the collaboration.

If you're a group organiser, work in whatever way you think best. If you want to work with us, ask; we'd love to hear from you.

[37] And yes, there's a Freudian subtext too.

What Next For You?

And gentlemen in England now a-bed

Shall think themselves accurs'd they were not here,

And hold their manhoods cheap whiles any speaks

That fought with us upon Saint Crispin's day.

- William Shakespeare, Henry V

"It is all around us, even now, in this very room. You can see it when you look out your window, or when you turn on your television. You can feel it when you go to work. When you go to church. When you pay your taxes. It is the world that has been pulled over your eyes to blind you from the truth.

"That you are a slave, Neo. Like everyone else, you were born into bondage, born into a prison that you cannot smell or taste or touch. A prison for your mind.

"Unfortunately, no one can be told what the Matrix is. You have to see it for yourself. This is your last chance. After this there is no turning back.

"You take the Blue Pill. The story ends, and you wake up in your bed and believe whatever you want to believe.

"You take the Red Pill, and you stay in Wonderland, and I show you how deep the rabbit hole goes."

The 1999 film, The Matrix, has a key scene where the protagonist, Neo, is given the choice: take the Blue Pill and return to the illusion of the world that he's accepted all his life, and go on as before. Or the Red Pill: do something about it.

Being a hero, Neo takes the Red Pill. You don't have to be a hero; we're advocating sustainable activism. But don't take the Blue Pill. This isn't sci-fi; unless we change the destructive way we allow our economies to be run, we face serious environmental crises, ever mounting wealth inequality and debt problems, more wars, and the continued squandering of human potential.

If you're already an activist: thank you! Keep it up, try new things, and use some of the ideas in this book if you like them. We'd be even happier if you gave us a name check.

If you're someone who, like Neo, knew there was something wrong with the world, but didn't know where to start: welcome! Join a group, find some people you like, and take it from there. Get in touch, if you like[38]. But don't stay at home

[38] Check out the list of contacts at the back of the book

shouting at the TV. Do something, and connect with other people, both online and in person. To quote the Matrix again:

> Sooner or later you're going to realise, just like we did, there's a difference between knowing the path, and walking the path.

All that is required for evil to succeed

is that good people do nothing.

ACKNOWLEDGEMENTS

This book was written in a hurry, between the end of the general election of June 2017 and the start of August 2017, so we could get it printed in time for September's The World Transformed festival, of which we were one of the founders.

It's traditional when writing acknowledgements to humbly add the phrase: "any errors are my own". In this case it's not false humility, it's true, and there are probably a lot more than there would be if we'd had time to go through a full proof reading and editing process. But as we like to say: done is better than perfect. We'll learn from it, and improve upon it for the next volume.

So Jamie and Rachel would like to thank the following people who have helped us build Talk Socialism.

All the authors and researchers whose work we have so ruthlessly pillaged and mangled in order to make it fit into an 800 word chapter.

All the activists and Labour councillors and MPs who've helped us with our workshops, and all the participants in our reading groups. And all the people who've helped us on the way: Arman Esfandiari, Ramin Esfandiari, Judy Pearce, Chris Thornton, Charlotte Austin, and Gavin Thompson.

The awesomely organised Nadia Idle, for her encouragement and support on Operation Hedgehog, and being able to make a striving for professionalism fun. To all the Hedgehogs who have given us their time and attention.

Adam Klug and Emma Rees, for doing so much to make participatory politics a reality, along with Beth Foster Ogg and Santiago Bell Bradford. Roland Singer Kingsmith and the rest of the TWT team, especially Joe Todd, Ruairidh Paton, Charlie Clarke and Deborah Hermans.

Ken Loach, for taking a chance and working with a bunch of unknowns on experimental workshops; Ken, you're one of the nicest people we've ever worked with.

All the Talk Socialism team: as well as Jamie and Rachel, there's Carl Kennedy, whose drive and creativity through those early experiments in what makes a brilliant session have laid the foundations for much of our work, and his insight in understanding the profound link between beer and socialism. Master of savoir faire, Nick Arnold, who raises bonhomie to an art form. Connor Hodgson-Brunniche who comprehensively disproves the idea that young people have short attention spans. Gerry Byrne who proves Wittgenstein right [39]; and Julian Thompson, with his sense of the possible and ear for a good phrase. Finally, there's Michael Lloyd, who with his patience and sagacity, is that rarest of creatures: a professional economist who can communicate that the real purpose of economics is to avoid being deceived by economists.

As Jeremy Corbyn said, it's the families of those involved in politics who give so much. So an extra big thank you to Caroline, Leon and Nelson, who have had to put up with the leaking shower not being fixed because Jamie was too busy writing. The road to socialism will be paved with clean towels!

[39] If people never did silly things, nothing intelligent would ever get done.

CONTACT DETAILS OF ORGANISATIONS

There are loads of great organisations working for a better world. We're not going to attempt to list them, all, because we'd inevitably miss some off. So here's the websites of some of the ones we've worked with. Our details are at the front of the book.

Labour Party

www.labour.org.uk

Momentum

www.peoplesmomentum.com

War on Want

www.waronwant.org

The World Transformed

www.theworldtransformed.org

QUOTATIONS

The problem with quotes on the internet is you can't always verify their authenticity.

- Abraham Lincoln

If you believe Google, everything pithy was said by either Mark Twain or Albert Einstein. We have tried to verify all the quotes we've used. In some cases, no one seems to know. The ones below are unlikley to have been said by the person who is attributed; but rather than a big list of "Anonymous" we used the attribution that is most common, even though it is apocryphal.

I never teach my pupils. I only provide the conditions in which they can learn.

- Albert Einstein

Resentment is like drinking poison and then hoping it will kill your enemies.

- Nelson Mandela

It is the long history of humankind (and animal kind, too) those who learned to collaborate and improvise most effectively have prevailed.

- Charles Darwin

BIBLIOGRAPHY

Aristotle (long, long time ago) *Rhetoric*

Asch, S, E. (1963) *Effects of group pressure upon the modification and distortion of judgement,* Russell & Russell

Axelrod, R. (1984) *The Evolution of Cooperation*, Basic Books

Chang, H. J. (2010) *23 Things They Don't Tell You About Capitalism*, Penguin Group

Chang, H. J. (2014) *Economics: A User's Guide*, Penguin Group

Dawkins, R. (1976) *The Selfish Gene*, Oxford University Press

Festinger, L. (1957). *A Theory of Cognitive Dissonance*, Stanford University Press

Kahneman, D. (2011*) Thinking, Fast and Slow*, Stras and Giroux

Keen, S. (2011) *Debunking Economics*, Zed Books

Keynes, J. M. (1936) *The General Theory of Employment*, Interest and Money, Palgrave Macmillan

Keynes, J. M. (1963) *Economic Possibilities for our Grandchildren*, W. W. Norton & Co

Lewin, K. (1947) *Frontiers in Group Dynamics*

Marx, K. & Engles, F. (1848) *The Communist Manifesto*

Mason, P. M. (2015) *Postcapitalism A Guide to Our Future*, Allen Lane

Milgram, S. (1974) *Obedience to Authority*, Pinter & Martin Ltd

Minsky, H. (1992) *Financial Instability Hypothesis*, Levy Economics Institute

Nunes, T. et al (1993) *Street Mathematics and School Mathematics*, Cambridge University Press

Rogers, E. (1962) *Diffusion of Innovation*, Free Press

Piketty, T. (2014) *Capital in the Twenty-First Century*, Belknap Harvard

Polanyi, K. (1944) *The Great Transformation*, Victor Gollancz

Popper, K. (1934) *The Logic of Scientific Discovery*, as Logik der Forschung, English translation 1959

Ryan, R. M. & Deci, E. L (2017) *Self-Determination Theory*, London: The Guildford Press

Sloman, S. & Fernbach, P. (2017) *The Knowledge Illusion*, Macmillan

Surowiecki, J. (2004) *The Wisdom of Crowds*, Doubleday; Anchor

Thompson, E. P. (1963) *The Making of the English Working Class*, Victor Gollancz

Tuckman, B. W. (1965) Developmental sequence in small groups. *Psychological Bulletin*, 63, 384-399

Made in the USA
Middletown, DE
21 January 2018